BREAD BAKING FOR BEGINNERS

Delicious & Easy Bread Recipes for Perfect Homemade Bread

(Easy Bread Recipes, How to Bake a Delicious Bread)

Kathryn Lazar

Published by Alex Howard

© **Kathryn Lazar**

All Rights Reserved

Bread Baking For Beginners: Delicious & Easy Bread Recipes for Perfect Homemade Bread (Easy Bread Recipes, How to Bake a Delicious Bread)

ISBN 978-1-990169-32-8

All rights reserved. No part of this guide may be reproduced in any form without permission in writing from the publisher except in the case of brief quotations embodied in critical articles or reviews.

Legal & Disclaimer

The information contained in this book is not designed to replace or take the place of any form of medicine or professional medical advice. The information in this book has been provided for educational and entertainment purposes only.

The information contained in this book has been compiled from sources deemed reliable, and it is accurate to the best of the Author's knowledge; however, the Author cannot guarantee its accuracy and validity and cannot be held liable for any errors or omissions. Changes are periodically made to this book. You must consult your doctor or get professional medical advice before using any of the suggested remedies, techniques, or information in this book.

Table of contents

PART 1 9

- APPALACHIAN CORNBREAD 10
- BEST EVER BANANA BREAD 11
- 4H BANANA BREAD 12
- ALMOND & CRANBERRY COCONUT BREAD 13
- BACON PARMESAN POPOVERS 15
- BANANA BREAD 16
- BANANA NUTS BREAD... 18
- BANANA SOUR CREAM BREAD 20
- CLASSIC IRISH SODA BREAD 22
- BASIC FRUIT BREAD 24
- BEST HAWAIIAN BANANA NUT BREAD 26
- BLUEBERRY BANANA NUT BREAD... 29
- CATHY'S BANANA BREAD 31
- CHEESY GARLIC HERB QUICK BREAD 32
- CINNAMON RAISIN BREAD 33
- BANANA MAPLE NUT BREAD 34
- CRAN-ALMOND LOAF 35
- CINNAMON BREAD.. 37
- EINKORN BANANA BREAD 39
- CHOCOLATE QUICK BREAD 40
- CHOCOLATE CHAI MINI LOAVES... 41
- GLAZED CRANBERRY SWEET POTATO BREAD................................. 43
- CHOCOLATE YEAST BREAD.. 45
- APPLES AND BANANAS BREAD 47
- CANDY CANE CHOCOLATE 48
- COUNTRY CINNAMON SWIRL BREAD 50
- DOUBLE CRANBERRY BANANA BREAD 51
- FRENCH LOAVES 53
- CINNAMON SWIRL QUICK BREAD... 54
- CAST-IRON CHOCOLATE CHIP BANANA BREAD 55
- CRANBERRY ORANGE ALMOND BREAD 56
- CRESCENT ROLLS 57

Dutch Apple Loaf	60
Family Banana Nut Bread	61
Gluten-Free Vegan Banana Nut Bread	62
Banana Walnut Flax Seed Bread	63
Old-World Rye Bread	65
Cinnamon Raisin Bread	66
Lemony Zucchini Bread	68
Fresh Pear Bread	69
Orange-Chip Cranberry Bread	70
Chocolate Chip Cranberry Bread	71
Cinnamon Swirl Bread	73
Homemade English Muffin Bread	74
Rich Banana Bread	75
Herb Quick Bread	76
Pumpkin Bread	77
Garlic Bubble Loaf	79
Honey Spice Bread	81
Kiwi Bread	82
Chocolate Zucchini Bread	84
Crunchy Breadsticks	85
Gluten- And Dairy-Free Cinnamon Raisin Bread	86
Dinner Rolls	88
Lemon Blueberry Bread	90
Lemon-Thyme Tea Bread	92
Skillet Herb Bread	94
Mango-Banana Bread	95
Creamy Banana Bread	97
Honey-Spice Whole Wheat Banana Bread	98
Macadamia Nut	100
Extreme Banana Nut Bread	101
Ice Cream Bread	102
Maine Pumpkin Bread	103
Maple Banana Bread	104
Soft Onion Breadsticks	105
Eggnog Mini Loaves	107
Peach Cobbler Bread	108
Favorite Irish Bread	110

Monkey Bread 111
Moroccan Spiced Fruit & Nut Bread 112
One-Bowl Chocolate Chip Bread 114
Poppy Seed Bread With Orange Glaze 115
Grandma's Onion Squares 117
Parmesan Zucchini Bread 119
Pina Colada Zucchini Bread 121
Pistachio Quick Bread 122
Pumpkin Bread With Gingerbread Topping 123
High-Protein Banana Bread 125
Sweet Potato Cinnamon Bread 126
Pizza Dough 127
Pumpkin Banana Bread 128
Scottish Oatmeal Rolls 130
Skillet Cinnamon Rolls 131
Seeded Whole Grain Loaf 133
Sausage Casserole 135
Socca 137
Olive & Onion Quick Bread 138
Soda Bread 139
Soft Sesame Breadsticks 140
Spicy Applesauce Fruit Bread 141
Spinach Quiche 143
Strawberry Bread 145
Sweet Italian Holiday Bread 146
Swiss Beer Bread 147
Waffles 148
Whole Wheat Banana Bread 149
Whole Wheat Banana Nut Bread 150
Wholesome Wheat Bread 151
Zucchini Bread 152

PART 2 153

INTRODUCTION 154

Simple Cinnamon Bread 155
Date & Walnut Bread 156

- Chocolaty Banana Bread 157
- Chocolaty Avocado Bread 158
- Lemony Blueberry Bread 159
- Nutty Apple Bread 161
- Spiced Zucchini & Banana Bread 162
- Zucchini & Carrot Bread 164
- Spiced Pumpkin Bread 166
- Dried Fruit & Seeds Bread 168
- Nuts & Seeds Bread 170

DARK CARAWAY SEEDS BREAD 172

- Cheesy Pesto Bread 174
- Herbed Zucchini & Carrot Bread 176
- Bacon & Jalapeño Pepper Bread 178

HOMEMADE BREAD RECIPES 180

- Classic Sandwich Loaf 180
- Easy Banana Bread 182
- Homemade Whole Wheat Loaf 183
- Homemade Foccacia 184
- Dinner Rolls 185
- Homemade White Bread 186
- Zucchini And Walnut Loaf 187
- Homemade French Baguette 188
- Apple Walnut Loaf 189
- Homemade Ciabatta 190
- Western Fried Bread 191
- Warm Dill Loaf 192
- Homemade Olive Bread Bites 193
- Melted Muenster Bun 194
- Mango Walnut Loaf 195
- Homemade Herbed Loaf 196
- Homemade Buttermilk Cornbread 197
- Honey Bun 198
- Cereal Wheat Breakfast Loaf 199
- Homemade Brown Bread 200

Part 1

Appalachian Cornbread

Servings: 9
Ingredients

 2 tablespoons chopped onions
 4 tablespoons canola oils , divided
 1 cup all-purpose flour
 1 cup cornmeal
 2 tablespoons sugar
 4 teaspoons baking powder
 1/2 teaspoon salt
 2 large eggs , room temperature
 1 cup whole milk
 1/2 cup fresh or frozen corn , thawed
 1/3 cup shredded Cheddar cheese
 1/4 cup salsa
 2 tablespoons minced chives

Directions

Preheat oven to 425°. In a tiny saucepan, saute onion in 1 tablespoon oil until tender; reserve.

In a huge bowl, incorporate flour, cornmeal, sugar, baking powder and salt. In another bowl, whisk eggs, milk and remaining oil. Stir in corn, cheese, salsa, chives and reserved onion. Stir in to the dry ingredients just until combined.

Transfer to a greased 9-in. square baking pan. Bake until a toothpick inserted in the guts comes out clean and top is lightly browned, 20-25 minutes. Cut into squares; serve warm.

Best Ever Banana Bread

Servings: 5
Ingredients

1 3/4 cups 1-3/4 all-purpose flour
1 1/2 cups 1-1/2 sugar
1 teaspoon baking soda
1/2 teaspoon salt
2 large eggs , room temperature
2 medium ripe bananas , mashed (1 cup)
1/2 cup canola oil
1/4 cup plus 1 tablespoon buttermilk
1 teaspoon vanilla extract
1 cup chopped walnuts

Directions

Preheat oven to 350°. In a huge bowl, stir together flour, sugar, baking soda and salt. In another bowl, incorporate the eggs, bananas, oil, buttermilk and vanilla; increase flour mixture, stirring just until combined. Fold in nuts.

Pour right into a greased or parchment-lined 9x5-in. loaf pan. If desired, sprinkle with additional walnuts. Bake until a toothpick comes out clean, 1-1/4 to 1-1/2 hours. Cool in pan for quarter-hour before removing to a wire rack.

4h Banana Bread

Servings: 5
Ingredients

2 cups all-purpose flour
1/2 teaspoon baking soda
1 cup white sugar
1 egg
5 tablespoons milk
1 teaspoon baking powder
1/2 teaspoon salt
1/2 cup margarine
1 cup mashed banana
1/2 cup chopped walnuts

Directions

1 Sift together flour, baking soda, baking powder, and salt.

2 In a sizable bowl, cream sugar and butter or margarine. Beat the egg slightly, and mix in to the creamed mixture with the bananas. Mix in sifted ingredients until just combined. Stir in milk and nuts. Spread batter into one greased and floured 9x5 inch loaf pan.

3 Bake at 350 degrees F (175 degrees C) until top is brown and cracks along the most notable.

Almond & Cranberry Coconut Bread

Servings: 2
Ingredients

2 cups sweetened shredded coconut
1 cup slivered almonds
1 cup butter , softened
1 cup sugar
4 large eggs , room temperature
1 cup vanilla yogurt
1 teaspoon almond extract
4 1/2 cups 4-1/2 all-purpose flour
3 teaspoons baking powder
1/2 teaspoon salt
1/2 teaspoon baking soda
1 can (15 ounces) cream of coconut
1 cup dried cranberries

Directions

Place coconut and almonds within an ungreased 15x10x1-in. pan. Bake at 350° for 10-15 minutes or until lightly toasted, stirring occasionally. Cool.

In a sizable bowl, cream butter and sugar until light and fluffy. Add eggs, individually, beating well after every addition. Beat in yogurt and extract until blended. Combine the flour, baking powder, salt and baking soda. Enhance the creamed mixture alternately with cream of coconut, beating well after every addition. Fold in the cranberries, coconut and almonds.

Transfer to two greased and floured 9x5-in. loaf pans. Bake at 350° for 60-70 minutes or until a toothpick inserted in the guts comes out clean. Cool for ten minutes before removing from pans to wire racks to cool completely.

Bacon Parmesan Popovers

Servings: 6

Ingredients

- 2 large eggs, room temperature
- 1 cup 2% milk
- 1 cup all-purpose flour
- 2 tablespoons grated Parmesan cheese
- 1/4 teaspoon salt
- 3 bacon strips, diced

Directions

In a sizable bowl, beat eggs and milk. Combine flour, cheese and salt; increase egg mixture and mix well. Cover and let stand at room temperature for 45 minutes.

Preheat oven to 450°. In a sizable skillet, cook bacon over medium heat until crisp. Utilizing a slotted spoon, remove to paper towels to drain. Grease cups of a nonstick popover pan well with a number of the bacon drippings; reserve. Stir bacon into batter; fill prepared cups two-thirds full.

Bake a quarter-hour. Reduce heat to 350° (usually do not open oven door). Bake a quarter-hour longer or until deep golden brown (usually do not underbake).

Run a table knife or small metal spatula around edges of cups to loosen if necessary. Immediately remove popovers from pan; prick with a tiny sharp knife to permit steam to flee. Serve immediately.

Banana Bread

Servings: 5
Ingredients

- 3 medium (7" to 7-7/8" long)s ripe bananas, mashed
- 1 cup white sugar
- 1 egg
- 1/4 cup melted butter
- 1 1/2 cups all-purpose flour
- 1 teaspoon baking soda
- 1 teaspoon salt

Directions

1 Preheat oven to 325 degrees F (165 degrees C). Grease a 9x5-inch loaf pan.

2 Combine bananas, sugar, egg, and butter together in a bowl. Mix flour and baking soda together in another bowl; stir into banana mixture until batter is merely mixed. Stir salt into batter. Pour batter in to the prepared loaf pan.

3 Bake in the preheated oven until a toothpick inserted in the heart of the bread comes out clean, about one hour.

Banana Nuts Bread

Servings: 2
Ingredients

1 1/2 cups all-purpose flour
1 teaspoon baking soda
1/2 teaspoon salt
1 cup white sugar
2 large eggs, beaten
1/4 cup butter, melted
3 medium (7" to 7-7/8" long)s bananas, mashed

Directions
1 Grease and flour two 7x3 inch loaf pans. Preheat oven to 350 degrees F (175 degrees C).

2 In a single bowl, whisk together flour, soda, salt, and sugar. Mix in slightly beaten eggs, melted butter, and mashed bananas. Stir in nuts if desired. Pour into prepared pans.

3 Bake at 350 degrees F (175 degrees C) for one hour, or until a wooden toothpick inserted in the guts comes out clean.

Banana Sour Cream Bread

Servings: 20
Ingredients

2 1/2 tablespoons white sugar
5/8 teaspoon ground cinnamon
1/2 cup butter
2 cups white sugar
1 7/8 eggs
3 3/4 very ripe bananas, mashed
5/8 (16-ounce) container sour cream
1 1/4 teaspoons vanilla extract
1 1/4 teaspoons ground cinnamon
5/16

teaspoon salt
1 7/8 teaspoons baking soda
2 3/4 cups all-purpose flour
2/3 cup chopped walnuts (optional)

Directions

Preheat oven to 300 degrees F (150 degrees C). Grease four 7x3 inch loaf pans. In a tiny bowl, stir together 1/4 cup white sugar and 1 teaspoon cinnamon. Dust pans lightly with cinnamon and sugar mixture.

In a sizable bowl, cream butter and 3 cups sugar. Mix in eggs, mashed bananas, sour cream, vanilla and cinnamon. Mix in salt, baking soda and flour. Stir in nuts. Divide into prepared pans.

Bake for one hour, until a toothpick inserted in center comes out clean.

Classic Irish Soda Bread

Servings: 6
Ingredients

1   1/2 cups all-purpose flour
1   1/2 tablespoons brown sugar
3/4 teaspoon baking powder
3/4 teaspoon baking soda
3/8 teaspoon salt
2 tablespoons cold butter, cubed
1 1/2 large eggs, room temperature, divided use
1/2 cup buttermilk
1/4 cup raisins

Directions

Preheat oven to 375°. Whisk together first 5 ingredients. Cut in butter until mixture resembles coarse crumbs. In another bowl, whisk together 1 egg and buttermilk. Increase flour mixture; stir just until moistened. Stir in raisins.

Turn onto a lightly floured surface; knead gently 6-8 times. Shape right into a 6-1/2-in. round loaf; put on a greased baking sheet. Utilizing a sharp knife, make a shallow cross in top of loaf. Whisk remaining egg; brush over top.

Bake until golden brown, 30-35 minutes. Remove from pan to a wire rack. Serve warm.

Basic Fruit Bread

Servings: 6
Ingredients

- 3 2/3 cups all-purpose flour
- 2 3/8 teaspoons baking powder
- 1 3/16 teaspoons baking soda
- 5/8 teaspoon salt
- 1 1/4 cups white sugar
- 2/3 cup vegetable oil
- 2 2/5 large eggs
- 1 1/4 cups shredded apples
- 1 cup chopped walnuts

5/8 teaspoon vanilla extract

Directions

1 Preheat oven to 350 degrees F (175 degrees C). Grease one 4 1/2 x 8 1/2 inch loaf pan.

2 Mix flour, baking powder, soda, salt, sugar, oil, eggs, apple, walnuts, and vanilla only until dry ingredients are moistened.

3 Bake in greased 4 1/2 x 8 1/2 inch loaf pan at 350 degrees F (175 degrees C) for 35 to 40 minutes.

Best Hawaiian Banana Nut Bread

Servings: 5
Ingredients

2 cups all-purpose flour
1 1/4 cups white sugar
1 tablespoon light brown sugar
3/4 teaspoon baking soda
3/4 teaspoon ground cinnamon
1/2 teaspoon baking powder
1/2 teaspoon salt
1 1/3 cups mashed bananas
2/3 cup canola oil
2/3 cup

crushed pineapple, drained

2/3 cup flaked coconut

1/4 cup chopped walnuts

1/4 cup chopped macadamia nut

2 large eggs, well beaten

4 teaspoons applesauce

1 1/2 teaspoons vanilla extract

1 teaspoon lemon extract

1/2 teaspoon coconut extract

2 tablespoons butter, at room temperature

1/4 cup white sugar

1/4 cup

chopped walnuts
1/4 cup chopped macadamia nut
1 teaspoon milk

Directions

1 Preheat oven to 350 degrees F (175 degrees C). Grease a 9x5-inch loaf pan.

2 Mix flour, 1 1/4 cup white sugar, brown sugar, baking soda, cinnamon, baking powder, and salt in a sizable bowl. Stir mashed banana, canola oil, pineapple, flaked coconut, 1/4 cup walnuts, 1/4 cup macadamia nuts, eggs, applesauce, vanilla extract, lemon extract, and coconut extract into flour mixture until blended. Pour batter into prepared loaf pan.

3 Bake in the preheated oven until a toothpick inserted in the heart of the loaf comes out clean, 70 to 80 minutes. Cool bread in the pan for ten minutes; remove and transfer to a wire rack to cool, 20 to thirty minutes.

4 Mix butter, 1/4 cup white sugar, 1/4 cup walnuts, 1/4 cup macadamia nuts, and milk together in a bowl. Spread along with bread once it's been used in the wire rack.

Blueberry Banana Nut Bread

Servings: 6
Ingredients

- 3/4 cup fresh blueberries
- 1 tablespoon cake flour
- 1/4 cup steel-cut oats
- 1/4 cup chopped pecans
- 3/4 cup cake flour
- 1 1/2 tablespoons cake flour
- 1/2 teaspoon baking soda
- 1/8 teaspoon salt
- 1/4 cup white sugar
- 1/4 cup brown sugar
- 2 tablespoons greek yogurt
- 2 tablespoons applesauce
- 1 large egg eggs
- 1/2 teaspoon vanilla extract
- 1/2 cup mashed banana
- 1 tablespoon cold butter
- 2 tablespoons brown sugar

Directions

1 Preheat oven to 350 degrees F (175 degrees C). Grease and flour a 4 1/2x8 1/2-inch loaf pan.

2 Stir and coat blueberries with 2 tablespoons cake flour in a bowl.

3 Mix coated blueberries, oats, pecans, 1 1/2 cups plus 3 tablespoons cake flour, baking soda, and salt in a bowl.

4 Beat white sugar, 1/2 cup brown sugar, Greek yogurt, and applesauce together in a sizable bowl until light and fluffy. Add eggs, individually; beat after every addition. Add vanilla extract and mashed banana; beat lightly until well blended.

5 Stir blueberry-flour mixture into yogurt mixture until just moistened. Spoon batter into prepared pan. Cut butter into 1/4 cup brown sugar in a tiny bowl until crumbly; sprinkle over batter.

about 55 minutes. Cool in the pan for a quarter-hour; remove from pan and cool on wire rack for one hour.

Cathy's Banana Bread

Servings: 3

Ingredients

- 1 cup mashed banana
- 1 cup sour cream
- 1/4 cup margarine
- 1 1/3 cups white sugar
- 2 large eggs
- 1 teaspoon vanilla extract
- 2 cups all-purpose flour
- 1 teaspoon baking soda
- 1 teaspoon baking powder
- 1/4 teaspoon salt

Directions

1 Preheat oven to 350 degrees F (175 degrees C). Grease and flour one 9x13 inch pan, or two 7x3 inch loaf pans.

2 Combine banana and sour cream. Reserve. In a huge bowl, cream together the margarine and sugar until smooth. Beat in the eggs individually, then stir in the vanilla and banana mixture. Combine the flour, baking soda, baking powder and salt; stir in to the banana mixture. Spread the batter evenly in to the prepared pan or pans.

3 Bake for 50 minutes in the preheated oven, or until a toothpick inserted in to the center of the bread comes out clean.

Cheesy Garlic Herb Quick Bread

Servings: 5
Ingredients

3 cups all-purpose flour
3 tablespoons sugar
1 tablespoon baking powder
2 teaspoons Italian seasoning
1 teaspoon garlic powder
1/2 teaspoon salt
1 large egg , room temperature
1 cup fat-free milk
1/3 cup canola oil
1 cup shredded sharp Cheddar cheese

Directions

Preheat oven to 350°. In a huge bowl, whisk together first 6 ingredients. In another bowl, whisk together egg, milk and oil. Stir in cheese and increase flour mixture; stir just until moistened.

Spoon batter right into a greased 9-in. cast-iron skillet and bake at 350° until a toothpick inserted in center comes out clean, 25-30 minutes.

Cinnamon Raisin Bread

Servings: 4
Ingredients

8 cups all-purpose flour
4 cups sugar , divided
1 1/2 tablespoons baking soda
2 teaspoons salt
4 large eggs , room temperature
4 cups buttermilk
1 cup canola oil
1 cup raisins
2 tablespoons ground cinnamon

Directions

Preheat oven to 350°. In a sizable bowl, incorporate flour, 1-1/2 cups sugar, soda and salt. In a tiny bowl, whisk eggs, buttermilk and oil. Stir into dry ingredients just until moistened. Fold in raisins. Combine cinnamon and remaining sugar; reserve.

Spoon half the batter into 2 greased 8x4-in. loaf pans. Sprinkle with half of the reserved cinnamon sugar; repeat layers. Cut through batter with a knife to swirl.

Bake 55-60 minutes or until a toothpick inserted in center comes out clean. Cool ten minutes before removing from pans to wire racks. Freeze option: Wrap cooled bread in foil and freeze for three months. To use, thaw at room temperature.

Banana Maple Nut Bread

Servings: 6
Ingredients

2 1/3 cups whole wheat flour
5/16 teaspoon salt
2/3 cup vegetable oil
2/3 cup pure maple syrup
4 4/5 large eggs, separated
2 1/2 tablespoons milk
3 3/5 medium (7" to 7-7/8" long)s bananas, mashed
2/3 cup chopped walnuts

Directions

1 Preheat oven to 350 degrees F (175 degrees C). Lightly grease a 9x5 inch loaf pan.

2 In a huge mixing bowl, incorporate flour and salt. Add oil, syrup and egg yolks; stir well. Add milk and mashed bananas; stir well. Add chopped nuts and stir.

3 Beat egg whites until stiff; fold into batter. Pour batter into prepared loaf pan. Bake at 350 degrees F (175 degrees C) for 50 minutes, or until a toothpick inserted into center of the loaf comes out clean.

Cran-Almond Loaf

Servings: 5
Ingredients

- 2 cups all-purpose flour
- 1 cup sugar
- 1 teaspoon salt
- 1/2 teaspoon baking soda
- 1/2 teaspoon baking powder
- 1/2 teaspoon ground nutmeg
- 2 large eggs
- 1 cup buttermilk
- 1/3 cup canola oil
- 1/4 teaspoon almond extract

1 cup dried cranberries, chopped

Directions

Preheat oven to 350°. Whisk together the first six ingredients. In another bowl, whisk together eggs, buttermilk, oil and extract. Increase flour mixture; stir just until moistened. Fold in cranberries.

Transfer to a greased 9x5-in. loaf pan. Bake until a toothpick inserted in center comes out clean, 60-65 minutes. Cool in pan ten minutes before removing to a wire rack to cool.

Cinnamon Bread

Servings: 5
Ingredients

2 cups all-purpose flour
1 cup white sugar
2 teaspoons baking powder
1/2 teaspoon baking soda
1 1/2 teaspoons ground cinnamon
1 teaspoon salt
1 cup buttermilk
1/4 cup vegetable oil
2 large eggs
2 teaspoons vanilla extract
2 tablespoons white sugar
1 teaspoon ground cinnamon
2 teaspoons margarine

Directions

1 Preheat oven to 350 degrees F (175 degrees C). Grease one 9x5 inch loaf pan.

2 Measure flour, 1 cup sugar, baking powder, baking soda, 1 1/2 teaspoons cinnamon, salt, buttermilk, oil, eggs and vanilla into large mixing bowl. Beat three minutes. Pour into prepared loaf pan. Smooth top.

3 Combine 2 tablespoons white sugar, 1 teaspoon cinnamon and butter, mixing until crumbly. Sprinkle topping over smoothed batter. Using knife, cut in a light swirling motion to provide a marbled effect.

4 Bake for approximately 50 minutes. Test with toothpick. When inserted it will turn out clean. Remove bread from pan to rack to cool.

Einkorn Banana Bread

Servings: 6
Ingredients

1/4 cup butter , melted
1/2 cup white sugar
1 large egg eggs
1 1/2 teaspoons milk
1/2 teaspoon vanilla extract
3/4 cup all-purpose einkorn flour, sifted
1/2 teaspoon ground cinnamon
1/2 teaspoon baking soda
1/2 teaspoon baking powder
1/8 teaspoon salt
1/4 cup chopped walnuts
1 1/2 medium (7" to 7-7/8" long) ripe bananas

Directions

1 Preheat the oven to 350 degrees F (175 degrees C). Grease a 9x5-inch loaf pan.

2 Stir melted butter and sugar together in a bowl. Add eggs, milk, and vanilla extract and mix well.

3 Combine sifted einkorn flour, cinnamon, baking soda, baking powder, and salt in another bowl. Stir in to the butter mixture until smooth. Fold walnuts and mashed bananas in to the batter until well mixed. Spread batter evenly in to the prepared pan.

4 Bake in the preheated oven until an instant-read thermometer inserted in to the center of the loaf reads 195 degrees F (90 degrees C), about 55 minutes. Cool loaf in the pan for ten minutes, then remove from the pan and transfer to a wire rack until completely cooled.

Chocolate Quick Bread

Servings: 6
Ingredients

2 cups 1-3/4 all-purpose flour
2/3 cup baking cocoa
5/8 teaspoon baking powder
5/8 teaspoon baking soda
5/8 teaspoon salt
2/3 cup butter, softened
1 1/4 cups sugar
2 2/5 large eggs, room temperature
1 1/4 cups buttermilk
2/3 cup miniature semisweet chocolate chips
6 1/2 tablespoons chopped pecans

Directions

In a huge bowl, incorporate the flour, cocoa, baking powder, baking soda and salt. In a huge bowl, cream butter and sugar until light and fluffy, 5-7 minutes. Add eggs, 1 at the same time, beating well after every addition. Add buttermilk; mix well. Stir into dry ingredients just until moistened. Fold in chocolate chips and pecans.

Pour right into a greased 9x5-in. loaf pan. Bake at 350° for 55-60 minutes or until a toothpick inserted in the guts comes out clean. Cool for ten minutes before removing from pan to a wire rack to cool completely.

Chocolate Chai Mini Loaves

Servings: 4
Ingredients

- 2 2/3 ounces semisweet chocolate, chopped
- 2/3 cup water
- 2/3 cup butter, softened
- 1 1/3 cups packed brown sugar
- 2 2/3 large eggs, room temperature
- 1 1/3 teaspoons vanilla extract
- 2 cups 1-1/2 all-purpose flour
- 1/4 cup chai tea latte mix
- 1 1/3 teaspoons baking soda
- 2/3 teaspoon salt
- 2/3 cup sour cream
- frosting:
- 1 1/3 cups confectioners' sugar
- 1 1/2 tablespoons butter, softened
- 1 1/2 tablespoons chai tea latte mixes
- 2/3 teaspoon vanilla extract
- 5 1/3 teaspoons whole milk

Directions

In a microwave, melt chocolate with the water; stir until smooth. Cool slightly. In a huge bowl, cream butter and brown sugar until light and fluffy. Add 1 egg at the same time, beating well after every addition. Beat in vanilla, then chocolate mixture.

Combine the flour, latte mix, baking soda and salt; increase creamed mixture alternately with sour cream.

Transfer to 3 greased 5-3/4x3x2-in. loaf pans. Bake at 350° for 35-40 minutes or until a toothpick inserted in the guts comes out clean. Cool for ten minutes before removing from pans to a wire rack to cool completely.

For frosting, incorporate the confectioners' sugar, butter, latte mix, vanilla and enough milk to accomplish desired consistency. Frost tops of loaves.

Glazed Cranberry Sweet Potato Bread

Servings: 2

Ingredients

3 1/2 cups 3-1/2 all-purpose flour
1 2/3 cups 1-2/3 sugar
2 teaspoons baking soda
2 teaspoons pumpkins pie spice
1 teaspoon baking powder
3/4 teaspoon salt
4 large eggs , lightly beaten, room temperature
2 cups mashed cooked sweet potatoes
1 can (14 ounces) whole-berry cranberry sauce
2/3 cup canola oil
3/4 cup chopped pecans
glaze:
1 cup confectioners' sugar
1/4 cup orange juice concentrate
1/8 teaspoon ground allspice

Directions

In a sizable bowl, incorporate the flour, sugar, baking soda, pie spice, baking powder and salt. In another large bowl, incorporate the eggs, sweet potatoes, cranberry sauce and oil. Stir into dry ingredients just until moistened. Fold in pecans.

Pour into 2 greased 9x5-in. loaf pans. Bake at 350° until a toothpick inserted in the guts comes out clean, about 55-60 minutes. Cool for ten minutes before removing from pans to wire racks to cool completely. In a tiny bowl, incorporate the glaze ingredients until smooth; drizzle over cooled loaves.

Chocolate Yeast Bread

Servings: 4
Ingredients

- 9 cups 4-1/2 all-purpose flour
- 2/3 cup baking cocoa
- 1/4 cup sugar
- 2 packages (1/4 ounce) active dry yeast
- 2 teaspoons salt
- 1/2 teaspoon baking soda
- 2 cups water
- 1 cup whole milk
- 1 cup semisweet chocolate chips
- 1/4 cup butter
- 2 large eggs, room temperature
- optional: baking cocoa and/or confectioners' sugar

Directions

In a bowl, incorporate 1-1/4 cups flour, cocoa, sugar, yeast, salt and baking soda. In a saucepan, heat the water, milk, chocolate chips and butter; stir until chocolate is melted. Cool to 120°-130°. Increase dry ingredients; beat on medium speed for 2 minutes. Add 1/2 cup flour and egg; beat on high for 2 minutes. Stir in enough remaining flour to create a stiff dough.

Turn onto a floured surface; knead until smooth and elastic, 6-8 minutes. Place in a greased bowl, turning once to grease top. Cover and let rise in a warm place until doubled, about one hour.

Punch dough down. Turn onto a lightly floured surface; divide in two. Shape into loaves. Place in 2 greased 8x4-in. loaf pans. Cover and let rise until doubled, about one hour.

Bake at 375° until browned, 25-30 minutes. Remove from pans to cool on wire racks. Dust with baking cocoa or confectioners' sugar if desired

Apples And Bananas Bread

Servings: 6
Ingredients

1 3/4 cups 1-1/2 mashed ripe bananas (4-5 medium)
1 3/4 cups 1-1/2 chopped peeled apples (2 medium)
2/3 cup sugar
2/3 cup packed brown sugar
2 1/2 tablespoons water
2 1/2 tablespoons butter , melted
1 3/4 cups 1-1/2 all-purpose flour
1 3/16 teaspoons baking soda
1 3/16 teaspoons baking powder
5/16 teaspoon salt
1 1/4 cups sweetened shredded coconut
2/3 cup caramel sundae syrup
5/16 teaspoon sea salt

Directions

Preheat oven to 350°. Combine bananas, apples, sugars and water. Stir in melted butter. In another bowl, whisk flour, baking soda, baking powder and salt. Stir into banana mixture. Transfer to a greased and floured 9x5-in. loaf pan.

Bake until a toothpick inserted in center comes out clean, 50-60 minutes. Cool in pan ten minutes before removing to a wire rack to cool completely.

Meanwhile, toast coconut, stirring occasionally, in a shallow pan at 350° until golden brown, 4-6 minutes. Cool slightly. Mix coconut with caramel syrup and sea salt; spread over loaf.

Candy Cane Chocolate

Servings: 4
Ingredients

1/4 cup butter, softened
1 2/3 cups 1-2/3 packed brown sugar
4 large egg whites, room temperature
2 large eggs, room temperature
3/4 cup strong brewed coffee
1/2 cup vanilla yogurt
1/4 cup canola oil
1 tablespoon vanilla extract
1/4 teaspoon peppermint extract
3 1/2 cups 3-1/2 all-purpose flour
3/4 cup baking cocoa
1 1/2 teaspoons 1-1/2 baking soda
1/2 teaspoon salt
1 1/2 cups 1-1/2 buttermilk
1 cup miniature

semisweet chocolate chips

topping:
2 ounces white baking chocolate, melted
3 tablespoons crushed candy canes

Directions

Preheat oven to 350°. Coat eight 5-3/4x3x2-in. loaf pans with cooking spray. In a sizable bowl, beat butter and brown sugar until crumbly, about 2 minutes. Add egg whites, eggs, coffee, yogurt, oil and extracts until blended.

In another bowl, whisk flour, cocoa, baking soda and salt; increase brown sugar mixture alternately with buttermilk, beating well after every addition. Fold in chocolate chips.

Transfer to prepared pans. Bake until a toothpick inserted in center comes out clean, 35-40 minutes. Cool ten minutes before removing from pans to wire racks to cool completely.

Drizzle melted white baking chocolate over loaves. Sprinkle with crushed candies.

Country Cinnamon Swirl Bread

Servings: 5
Ingredients

- 1/4 cup butter , softened
- 1 1/3 cups 1-1/3 sugar , divided
- 1 large egg , room temperature
- 2 cups all-purpose flour
- 1 teaspoon baking powder
- 1/2 teaspoon baking soda
- 1/2 teaspoon salt
- 1 cup buttermilk
- 1 tablespoon ground cinnamon

Directions

In a sizable bowl, beat the butter, 1 cup sugar and egg until blended. Combine the flour, baking powder, baking soda and salt; increase egg mixture alternately with buttermilk. In a tiny bowl, incorporate the cinnamon and remaining sugar.

Pour a third of the batter right into a greased 8x4-in. loaf pan; sprinkle with a third of the cinnamon sugar. Repeat layers twice. Bake at 350° for 45-50 minutes or until a toothpick inserted in the guts comes out clean. Cool for ten minutes before removing from pan to a wire rack to cool completely.

Double Cranberry Banana Bread

Servings: 4
Ingredients

1/3 cup shortening
2/3 cup sugar
2 large eggs, room temperature
1 cup mashed ripe banana
1 teaspoon vanilla extract
1 3/4 cups 1-3/4 all-purpose flour
2 teaspoons baking powder
1/2 teaspoon salt
1/4 teaspoon baking soda
1 cup whole-berry cranberry sauce
3/4 cup chopped pecans, divided
1/2 cup dried cranberries

Directions

Preheat oven to 350°. In a big bowl, cream shortening and sugar until light and crumbly. Beat in eggs, banana and vanilla. In another bowl, whisk flour, baking powder, salt and baking soda; gradually beat into creamed mixture. Stir in cranberry sauce, 1/2 cup pecans and dried cranberries.

Transfer to a greased 8x4-in. loaf pan. Sprinkle with remaining pecans. Bake until a toothpick inserted in center comes out clean, 50-60 minutes. Cool in pan 10 minutes before removing to a wire rack to cool completely.

Freeze option: Securely wrap cooled loaf in foil, then freeze. To use, thaw at room temperature.

French Loaves

Servings: 2
Ingredients

- 2 tablespoons active dry yeast
- 2 cups warm water (110° to 115°)
- 2 teaspoons salt
- 1 teaspoon sugar
- 4 1/2 to 5 4-1/2 to 5 cups bread flour
- 1 teaspoon cornmeal

Directions

In a huge bowl, dissolve yeast in tepid to warm water. Add salt, sugar and 2 cups flour. Beat until smooth. Stir in enough remaining flour to create a soft dough.

Turn onto a floured surface; knead until smooth and elastic, about 6-8 minutes. Place in a greased bowl, turning once to grease the very best. Cover and let rise in a warm place until doubled, about one hour.

Punch dough down. Turn onto a lightly floured surface; divide in two. Shape into 12-in.-long loaves.

Place seam side down on a greased baking sheet. Cover and let rise until doubled, about thirty minutes.

Preheat oven to 450°. Sprinkle loaves with cornmeal. With a sharp knife, make four shallow slashes over the top of every loaf. Bake 15-20 minutes or until golden brown. Cool on a wire rack.

Cinnamon Swirl Quick Bread

Servings: 5
Ingredients

2 cups all-purpose flour
1 1/2 cups 1-1/2 sugar , divided
1 teaspoon baking soda
1/2 teaspoon salt
1 cup buttermilk
1 large egg , room temperature
1/4 cup canola oil
3 teaspoons ground cinnamon
glaze:
1/4 cup confectioners' sugar
1 1/2 to 2 1-1/2 to 2 teaspoons whole milk

Directions

Preheat oven to 350°. In a sizable bowl, incorporate flour, 1 cup sugar, baking soda and salt. Combine buttermilk, egg and oil; stir into dry ingredients just until moistened. In a tiny bowl, incorporate cinnamon and remaining sugar.

Grease underneath only of a 9x5-in. loaf pan. Pour half the batter into pan; sprinkle with half the cinnamon-sugar. Carefully spread with remaining batter and sprinkle with remaining cinnamon-sugar; cut through batter with a knife to swirl.

Bake 45-50 minutes or until a toothpick inserted in center comes out clean. Cool ten minutes before removing from pan to a wire rack to cool completely. Combine confectioners' sugar and enough milk to attain desired consistency; drizzle over loaf.

Cast-Iron Chocolate Chip Banana Bread

Servings: 8
Ingredients

3 tablespoons butter , softened
3/4 cup sugar
4/5 large egg , room temperature
2 2/5 medium ripe bananas , mashed (about 1-1/4 cups)
13/16 teaspoon vanilla extract
1 2/3 cups all-purpose flour
13/16 teaspoon baking soda
3/8 teaspoon salt
3/4 cup semisweet chocolate chips, divided

Directions

Preheat oven to 350°. In a huge bowl, beat butter and sugar until crumbly. Beat in egg, bananas and vanilla. In another bowl, whisk flour, baking soda and salt; little by little beat into banana mixture. Stir in 1/2 cup chocolate chips.

Transfer to a greased 10-in. cast-iron or other ovenproof skillet; sprinkle with remaining 1/2 cup chocolate chips. Bake until a toothpick inserted in center comes out clean, 25-30 minutes. Cool in pan on a wire rack.

Cranberry Orange Almond Bread

Servings: 5
Ingredients

- 3 cups all-purpose flour
- 3 tablespoons sugar
- 1 tablespoon baking powder
- 1/2 teaspoon salt
- 1 cup dried cranberries
- 1/2 cup sliced almonds , toasted
- 1 large egg , room temperature
- 1 cup fat-free milk
- 1/3 cup canola oil
- 3/4 teaspoon grated orange zest
- 3/4 teaspoon almond extract

Directions

Preheat oven to 350°. In a sizable bowl, whisk together first 4 ingredients; stir in cranberries and almonds. In another bowl, whisk together egg, milk, oil, zest and extract. Increase flour mixture; stir just until moistened.

Transfer to a 9x5-in. loaf pan coated with cooking spray. Bake until a toothpick inserted in center comes out clean, 40-50 minutes. Cool in pan ten minutes before removing to a wire rack to cool.

Crescent Rolls

Servings: 16
Ingredients

1 1/2 3-3/4 to 4-1/4 cups all-purpose flour
1 package (1/4 ounce each) active dry yeast
1/2 teaspoon salt
1/2 cup whole milk
1/4 cup butter , cubed
2 tablespoons honey
1 1/2 large eggs yolks
1 tablespoon butter , melted

Directions

Preheat oven to 350°. In a big bowl, whisk together first 4 ingredients; stir in cranberries and almonds. In another bowl, whisk together egg, milk, oil, zest and extract. Increase flour mixture; stir just until moistened.

Transfer to a 9x5-in. loaf pan coated with cooking spray. Bake until a toothpick inserted in center comes out clean, 40-50 minutes. Cool in pan 10 minutes before removing to a wire rack to cool. Combine 1-1/2 cups flour, yeast and salt. In a tiny saucepan, heat milk, cubed butter and honey to 120°-130°. Increase dry ingredients; beat on medium speed 2 minutes. Add egg yolks; beat on high 2 minutes. Stir in enough remaining flour to create a soft dough (dough will be sticky).

Turn dough onto a floured surface; knead until smooth and elastic, 6-8 minutes. Place in a greased bowl, turning once to grease the very best. Cover and let rise in a warm place until doubled, about 45 minutes.

Punch down dough. Cover and refrigerate overnight.

To bake, turn dough onto a lightly floured surface; divide in two. Roll each portion right into a 14-in. circle; cut each circle into 16 wedges. Lightly brush wedges with melted butter. Roll-up from wide ends, pinching pointed ends to seal. Place 2 in. apart on parchment paper-lined baking sheets, point side down. Cover with lightly greased plastic wrap; let rise in a warm place until doubled, about 45 minutes.

Preheat oven to 375°. Bake until golden brown, 9-11 minutes. Remove from pans to wire racks; serve warm. Freeze option: Soon after shaping, freeze rolls on parchment paper-lined baking sheets until firm. Transfer to a resealable plastic bag; go back to freezer. Freeze up to four weeks. To use, let rise and bake as directed, increasing rise time to 2-1/2 to 3 hour

Caraway Cheese Bread

Servings: 6
Ingredients

- 3 cups 2-1/2 all-purpose flour
- 2 1/3 cups shredded Cheddar cheese
- 1 1/5 1-1/2 to 2 teaspoons caraway seeds
- 7/8 teaspoon salt
- 5/8 teaspoon baking powder
- 5/8 teaspoon baking soda
- 2 2/5 large eggs, room temperature
- 1 1/4 cups plain yogurt
- 2/3 cup butter, melted
- 1 tablespoon dijon mustard

Directions

Preheat oven to 375°. In a huge bowl, incorporate the first 6 ingredients. In another bowl, incorporate remaining ingredients. Stir into dry ingredients just until moistened.

Pour right into a greased 9x5-in. loaf pan. Bake until a toothpick comes out clean, 30-35 minutes. Cool ten minutes before removing from pan to a wire rack. Serve warm. Refrigerate leftovers.

Dutch Apple Loaf

Servings: 5
Ingredients

1/2 cup butter , softened
1 cup sugar
2 large eggs , room temperature
1/4 cup buttermilk
1 teaspoon vanilla extract
2 cups all-purpose flour
1 1/2 teaspoons 1-1/2 baking powder
1/2 teaspoon salt
1/4 teaspoon baking soda
2 cups diced peeled tart apples
1/2 cup chopped walnuts
topping:
1/4 cup sugar
1/4 cup all-purpose flour
2 teaspoons ground cinnamon
1/4 cup cold butter , cubed

Directions

In a big bowl, cream butter and sugar until light and fluffy. Add eggs, individually, beating well after each addition. Beat in buttermilk and vanilla. Combine the flour, baking powder, salt and baking soda; gradually increase creamed mixture. Fold in apples and walnuts. Pour in to a greased 9x5-in. loaf pan.

For topping, incorporate the sugar, flour and cinnamon. Cut in butter until mixture resembles coarse crumbs. Sprinkle over batter.

Bake at 350° for 55-60 minutes or until a toothpick inserted in the guts comes out clean. Cool for 10 minutes before removing from pan to a wire rack.

Family Banana Nut Bread

Servings: 6
Ingredients

1 1/5 (8-ounce) packages cream cheese, softened
1 1/4 cups white sugar
2/3 cup butter
2 2/5 eaches eggs, well-beaten
2 2/5 medium (7" to 7-7/8" long)s ripe bananas, mashed
2 2/3 cups all-purpose flour
1 13/16 teaspoons baking powder
5/8 teaspoon baking soda
1 1/4 cups chopped walnuts

Directions

1 Preheat an oven to 350 degrees F (175 degrees C). Grease a 9x5-inch loaf pan.

2 Beat together the cream cheese, sugar, butter, eggs, and banana in a huge bowl until very smooth. Stir in the flour, baking powder, baking soda, and walnuts until just combined. Pour the batter in to the prepared loaf pan.

Step about one hour and quarter-hour. Cool in the pan for ten minutes before removing to cool completely on a wire rack.

Gluten-Free Vegan Banana Nut Bread

Servings: 5
Ingredients

- 1 serving cooking spray
- 2 tablespoons boiling water
- 1 tablespoon flax seeds
- 1 cup mashed ripe banana
- 1/4 cup unsweetened applesauce
- 2 teaspoons vanilla extract
- 1 cup chopped medjool dates
- 1 cup oat flour
- 1/2 cup tapioca starch
- 4 teaspoons baking powder
- 1 teaspoon ground cinnamon
- 1/2 teaspoon baking soda
- 1/2 cup chopped walnuts

Directions

1 Preheat oven to 350 degrees F (175 degrees C). Grease a 9x5-inch loaf pan with cooking spray.

2 Mix boiling water and flax seeds together in a bowl.

3 Combine bananas, applesauce, and vanilla extract in the plate of a food processor; pulse until blended. Add dates slowly, as the food processor is running. Add flaxseed mixture and blend until smooth.

4 Mix oat flour, tapioca starch, baking powder, cinnamon, and baking soda in a huge bowl. Pour in banana mixture; mix well until a batter forms. Stir in walnuts. Pour batter in to the prepared loaf pan.

5 Bake in the preheated oven until a toothpick inserted in to the center comes out clean, 55 to 65 minutes. Cool on a wire rack.

Banana Walnut Flax Seed Bread

Servings: 2
Ingredients

2 cups whole wheat flour
1 cup flaxseed meal
1/4 cup wheat germ
2 teaspoons baking soda
1 teaspoon ground cinnamon
1/3 teaspoon sea salt
2 cups chopped walnuts
4 large eggs
2 cups brown sugar
2/3 cup sunflower seed oil
1/3 cup roasted walnut oil
1/4 cup plain yogurt
5 large ripe bananas , coarsely mashed, or more to taste
2 teaspoons vanilla extract

Directions

1 Preheat oven to 325 degrees F (165 degrees C). Butter two 8x4-inch loaf pans.

2 Whisk whole wheat, flaxseed meal, wheat germ, baking soda, cinnamon, and salt together in an enormous bowl. Stir walnuts into dry ingredients.

3 Beat eggs and brown sugar in another bowl with a power mixer until thick and pale, around three minutes. Add sunflower seed oil, walnut oil, and yogurt; beat to combine. Stir in mashed bananas and vanilla extract.

4 Pour egg mixture over dry ingredients and mix briefly, until just moistened. Divide batter between loaf pans.

5 Bake loaves in the preheated oven until a toothpick inserted into the centers comes out clean, about 1 hour and quarter-hour. Remove pans from the oven and let sit 5 minutes, then remove loaves to cool on wire racks.

Old-World Rye Bread

Servings: 2
Ingredients

2 packages (1/4 ounce each) active dry yeast
1 1/2 cups 1-1/2 warm water (110° to 115°)
1/2 cup molasses
6 tablespoons butter, softened
2 cups rye flour
1/4 cup baking cocoa
2 tablespoons caraway seeds
2 teaspoons salt
3 1/2 to 4 3-1/2 to 4 cups all-purpose flour
cornmeal

Directions

In a sizable bowl, dissolve yeast in hot water. Beat in the molasses, butter, rye flour, cocoa, caraway seeds, salt and 2 cups all-purpose flour until smooth. Stir in enough remaining all-purpose flour to create a stiff dough.

Turn onto a floured surface; knead until smooth and elastic, 6-8 minutes. Place in a greased bowl, turning once to grease top. Cover and let rise in a warm place until doubled, about 1-1/2 hours.

Punch dough down. Turn onto a lightly floured surface; divide in two. Shape each piece right into a loaf about 10 in. long. Grease 2 baking sheets and sprinkle with cornmeal. Place loaves on prepared pans. Cover and let rise until doubled, about one hour.

Bake at 350° for 35-40 minutes or until bread sounds hollow when tapped. Remove from pans to wire racks to cool.

Cinnamon Raisin Bread

Servings: 3
Ingredients

1 1/2 cups milk
1 cup warm water (110 degrees f/45 degrees c)
2 (.25 ounce) packages active dry yeast
3 large eggs
1/2 cup white sugar
1 teaspoon salt
1/2 cup margarine , softened
1 cup raisins
8 cups all-purpose flour
2 tablespoons milk
3/4 cup white sugar
2 tablespoons ground cinnamon
2 tablespoons butter , melted

Directions

1 Warm the milk in a tiny saucepan until it bubbles, then remove from heat. Let cool until lukewarm.

2 Dissolve yeast in tepid to warm water, and reserve until yeast is frothy. Mix in eggs, sugar, butter or margarine, salt, and raisins. Stir in cooled milk. Add the flour little by little to create a stiff dough.

3 Knead dough on a lightly floured surface for some minutes. Place in a big, greased, mixing bowl, and turn to grease the top of dough. Cover with a damp cloth. Allow to go up until doubled.

4 Roll from a lightly floured surface into a huge rectangle 1/2 inch thick. Moisten dough with 2 tablespoons milk. Mix together 3/4 cup sugar and 2 tablespoons cinnamon, and sprinkle mixture

along with the moistened dough. Roll-up tightly; the roll ought to be about 3 inches in diameter. Cut into thirds, and tuck under ends. Place loaves into well greased 9 x 5 inch pans. Lightly grease tops of loaves. Let rise again for one hour.

5 Bake at 350 degrees F (175 degrees C) for 45 minutes, or until loaves are lightly browned and sound hollow when knocked. Remove loaves from pans, and brush with melted butter or margarine. Let cool before slicing.

Lemony Zucchini Bread

Servings: 2
Ingredients

4 cups all-purpose flour
1 1/2 cups 1-1/2 sugar
1 package (3.4 ounces) instant lemon pudding mix
1 1/2 teaspoons 1-1/2 baking soda
1 teaspoon baking powder
1 teaspoon salt
4 large eggs , room temperature
1 1/4 cups 1-1/4 2% milk
1 cup canola oil
3 tablespoons lemon juice
1 teaspoon lemon extract
2 cups shredded zucchini
1/4 cup poppy seeds
2 teaspoons grated lemon zest

Directions

In a huge bowl, incorporate the flour, sugar, pudding mix, baking soda, baking powder and salt. In another bowl, whisk the eggs, milk, oil, lemon juice and extract. Stir into dry ingredients just until moistened. Fold in the zucchini, poppy seeds and lemon zest.

Pour into 2 greased 9x5-in. loaf pans. Bake at 350° for 50-55 minutes or until a toothpick inserted in the guts comes out clean. Cool for ten minutes before removing from pans to wire racks to cool completely.

Fresh Pear Bread

Servings: 2
Ingredients

3 large eggs , room temperature
1 1/2 cups 1-1/2 sugar
3/4 cup vegetable oil
1 teaspoon vanilla extract
3 cups all-purpose flour
2 teaspoons baking powder
2 teaspoons ground cinnamon
1 teaspoon baking soda
1 teaspoon salt
4 cups finely chopped peeled ripe pears (about 4 medium)
1 teaspoon lemon juice
1 cup chopped walnuts

Directions

In a bowl, incorporate the eggs, sugar, oil and vanilla; mix well. Combine flour, baking powder, cinnamon, baking soda and salt; stir in to the egg mixture just until moistened. Toss pears with lemon juice. Stir pears and walnuts into batter (batter will be thick).

Spoon into 2 greased 9x5-in. loaf pans. Bake at 350° for 55-60 minutes or until a toothpick inserted in the guts comes out clean. Cool for ten minutes before removing from pans to wire racks.

Orange-Chip Cranberry Bread

Servings: 2
Ingredients

2 1/2 cups 2-1/2 all-purpose flour
1 cup sugar
1/2 teaspoon baking powder
1/2 teaspoon baking soda
1/4 teaspoon salt
2 large eggs , room temperature
3/4 cup vegetable oil
2 teaspoons grated orange zest
1 cup buttermilk
1 1/2 cups 1-1/2 chopped fresh or frozen cranberries , thawed
1 cup miniature semisweet chocolate chips
1 cup chopped walnuts
3/4 cup confectioners' sugar , optional
2 tablespoons orange juice , optional

Directions

In a bowl, incorporate the first 5 ingredients. In another bowl, incorporate eggs, oil and orange zest; mix well. Increase dry ingredients alternately with buttermilk. Fold in cranberries, chocolate chips and walnuts.

Pour into 2 greased 8x4-in. loaf pans. Bake at 350° for 50-60 minutes or until a toothpick inserted in the guts comes out clean. Cool for ten minutes before removing from pans to wire racks. If glaze is desired, incorporate confectioners' sugar and orange juice until smooth; spread over cooled loaves.

Chocolate Chip Cranberry Bread

Servings: 5
Ingredients

2 cups all-purpose flour
3/4 cup sugar
2 teaspoons baking powder
1/2 teaspoon salt
1 large egg , room temperature
3/4 cup 2% milk
6 tablespoons butter , melted
1 cup fresh or frozen cranberries , halved
1 cup miniature semisweet chocolate chips
streusel:
1/3 cup packed brown sugar
2 tablespoons all-purpose flour
1/8 teaspoon ground cinnamon
2 tablespoons cold butter
3/4 cup confectioners' sugar
2 to 3 tablespoons whole milk

Directions

Preheat oven to 325°. Line bottom of a greased 9x5-in. loaf pan with parchment; grease parchment.

In a huge bowl, incorporate the flour, sugar, baking powder and salt. Whisk the egg, milk and butter; stir into dry ingredients just until moistened. Fold in cranberries and chocolate chips. Transfer to prepared pan.

In a tiny bowl, incorporate the brown sugar, flour and cinnamon; cut in butter until crumbly. Sprinkle over batter. Bake until a toothpick inserted in the guts comes out clean, 60-65 minutes.

Cool for ten minutes; loosen sides of bread from pan. Cool completely before removing from pan. For the glaze, mix confectioners' sugar and 2 tablespoons milk until smooth; if needed, add additional 1 tablespoon milk to attain desired consistency. Drizzle glaze over top of bread; allow to sit 10-15 minutes before slicing.

Cinnamon Swirl Bread

Servings: 5

Ingredients

- 1/3 cup white sugar
- 2 teaspoons ground cinnamon
- 2 cups all-purpose flour
- 1 tablespoon baking powder
- 1/2 teaspoon salt
- 1 cup white sugar
- 1 egg , beaten
- 1 cup milk
- 1/3 cup vegetable oil

Directions

1 Preheat oven to 350 degrees F (175 degrees C). Lightly grease a 9x5 inch loaf pan. In a tiny bowl, mix together 1/3 cup sugar and 2 teaspoons cinnamon; reserve.

2 In large bowl incorporate flour, baking powder, salt and remaining 1 cup sugar. Combine egg, milk, and oil; increase flour mixture. Stir until just moistened.

3 Pour half of the batter into pan. Sprinkle with half the reserved cinnamon/sugar mixture. Repeat with remaining batter and cinnamon/sugar mixture. Draw a knife through batter to marble.

4 Bake in preheated oven for 45 to 50 minutes, or until a toothpick inserted into center of the loaf comes out clean. Let cool in pan for ten minutes before removing to a wire rack to cool completely. Wrap in foil and let sit overnight before slicing.

Homemade English Muffin Bread

Servings: 2
Ingredients

5 cups all-purpose flour , divided
2 packages (1/4 ounce each) active dry yeast
1 tablespoon sugar
2 teaspoons salt
1/4 teaspoon baking soda
2 cups warm milk (110° to 115°)
1/2 cup warm water (120° to 130°)
cornmeal

Directions

In a huge bowl, incorporate 2 cups flour, yeast, sugar, salt and baking soda. Add warm milk and water; beat on low speed 30 seconds, scraping bowl occasionally. Beat on high three minutes. Stir in remaining flour (batter will be stiff). Usually do not knead.

Grease two 8x4-in. loaf pans. Sprinkle pans with cornmeal. Spoon batter into pans and sprinkle cornmeal at the top. Cover and let rise in a warm place until doubled, about 45 minutes.

Preheat oven to 375°. Bake 35 minutes or until golden brown. Remove from pans to wire racks to cool.

Rich Banana Bread

Servings: 5
Ingredients

1/2 cup butter , melted
1 cup white sugar
2 large eggs
1 teaspoon vanilla extract
1 1/2 cups all-purpose flour
1 teaspoon baking soda
1/2 teaspoon salt
1/2 cup sour cream
1/2 cup chopped walnuts
2 medium (7" to 7-7/8" long)s medium bananas , sliced

Directions

1 Preheat oven to 350 degrees F (175 degrees C). Grease a 9x5 inch loaf pan.

2 In a sizable bowl, stir together the melted butter and sugar. Add the eggs and vanilla, mix well. Combine the flour, baking soda and salt, stir in to the butter mixture until smooth. Finally, fold in the sour cream, walnuts and bananas. Spread evenly in to the prepared pan.

3 Bake at 350 degrees F (175 degrees C) for 60 minutes, or until a toothpick inserted in to the center of the loaf comes out clean. Cool loaf in the pan for ten minutes before removing to a wire rack to cool completely.

Herb Quick Bread

Servings: 5
Ingredients

3 cups all-purpose flour
3 tablespoons sugar
1 tablespoon baking powder
3 teaspoons caraway seeds
1/2 teaspoon salt
1/2 teaspoon ground nutmeg
1/2 teaspoon dried thyme
1 large egg
1 cup fat-free milk
1/3 cup canola oil

Directions

Preheat oven to 350°. In a huge bowl, whisk together first seven ingredients. In another bowl, whisk together egg, milk and oil. Increase flour mixture; stir just until moistened.

Transfer to a 9x5-in. loaf pan coated with cooking spray. Bake until a toothpick inserted in center comes out clean, 40-50 minutes. Cool in pan ten minutes before removing to a wire rack to cool.

Pumpkin Bread

Servings: 3
Ingredients

3 cups pumpkins canned pumpkin puree
1 <small>1/2</small> cup vegetable oil vegetable oil
4 cups sugar white sugar
6 eggs large eggs
4 <small>3/4</small> cups flour all-purpose flour
1 <small>1/2</small> teaspoon baking powder baking powder
1 <small>1/2</small> teaspoon baking soda baking soda
1 <small>1/2</small> teaspoon salt
1 <small>1/2</small> teaspoon ground cinnamon ground

cinnamon

1 1/2 teaspoon nutmeg

ground nutmeg

1 1/2 teaspoon cloves

ground cloves

Directions

1 Preheat the oven to 350 degrees F (175 degrees C). Grease and flour three 9x5 inch loaf pans.

2 In a sizable bowl, mix together the pumpkin, oil, sugar, and eggs. Combine the flour, baking powder, baking soda, salt, cinnamon, nutmeg, and cloves; stir in to the pumpkin mixture until well blended. Divide the batter evenly between your prepared pans.

3 Bake in preheated oven for 45 minutes to at least one 1 hour. The most notable of the loaf should spring when lightly pressed.

Garlic Bubble Loaf

Servings: 2
Ingredients

2 packages (1/4 ounce each) active dry yeast
1/4 cup warm water (110° to 115°)
2 cups warm whole milk (110° to 115°)
2 tablespoons sugar
1 tablespoon shortening
2 teaspoons salt
6 1/4 to 6 1/2 6-1/4 to 6-1/2 cups all-purpose flour
1/2 cup butter , melted
1 tablespoon dried parsley flakes
2 teaspoons garlic powder

Directions

In a huge bowl, dissolve yeast in tepid to warm water. Add the milk, sugar, shortening, salt and 2 cups flour; beat until smooth. Stir in enough of the rest of the flour to create a soft dough. Come out on a floured surface; knead until smooth and elastic, 6-8 minutes. Place in a greased bowl, turning once to grease top. Cover and let rise in a warm place until doubled, about one hour.

Punch dough down. Turn onto a lightly floured surface; divide into fourths. Divide each portion into 12 pieces. In a shallow bowl, incorporate the butter, parsley and garlic powder. Shape each piece right into a ball; dip in the butter mixture. Place in 2 grease 9x5-in. loaf pan. Pour any remaining butter mixture over dough. Cover and let rise until doubled, about thirty minutes.

Bake at 375° until golden brown, 35-40 minutes. Cool for ten minutes. Remove from pans to wire racks. Serve warm.

Honey Spice Bread

Servings: 5
Ingredients

- 2/3 cup packed brown sugar
- 1/3 cup 2% milk
- 2 cups all-purpose flour
- 1 1/2 teaspoons 1-1/2 baking powder
- 1/2 teaspoon ground cinnamon
- 1/2 teaspoon ground nutmeg
- 1/8 teaspoon ground cloves
- 2 large eggs
- 1/2 cup honey
- 1/3 cup canola oil
- glaze:
- 1/3 cup confectioners' sugar
- 2 teaspoons 2% milk

Directions

Preheat oven to 325°. In a tiny saucepan, incorporate brown sugar and milk. Cook and stir over low heat until sugar is dissolved. Remove from heat.

In a sizable bowl, whisk flour, baking powder, cinnamon, nutmeg and cloves. In another bowl, whisk eggs, honey, oil and brown sugar mixture until blended. Increase flour mixture; stir just until moistened.

Transfer to a greased 8x4-in. loaf pan. Bake 50-60 minutes or until a toothpick inserted in center comes out clean (cover top loosely with foil if had a need to prevent overbrowning).

Cool in pan ten minutes before removing to a wire rack to cool completely. In a tiny bowl, stir glaze ingredients until smooth; drizzle over bread. Freeze option: Securely wrap and freeze cooled loaf in plastic wrap and foil. To use, thaw at room temperature. Glaze as directed.

Kiwi Bread

Servings: 5
Ingredients

1 1/2 cups all-purpose flour
2 teaspoons baking powder
1/2 teaspoon salt
1 cup sugar
1/2 cup butter , melted and cooled
3 eggs
1/4 cup milk , divided
3/4 cup pureed kiwi fruit (about 4-5 kiwis)

Directions

Preheat oven to 350° F. Grease and line a 9x5-inch loaf pan with an extended strip parchment paper down the center with overhanging sides.

Prepare the kiwi puree by positioning peeled kiwi fruit in a food processor or blender. Blitz until no large chunks remain and you have a puree. Measure out 3/4 cup and reserve. If there's any remaining puree, use along with porridge for breakfast or eat immediately.

In a tiny bowl whisk together flour, baking powder, and salt.

In a sizable bowl or plate of a stand mixer, beat together melted butter and sugar, about 1 minute. Beat in eggs, individually, mixing well after every addition. Beat mixture until pale in color, about 2 minutes.

Add 1/2 of the flour mixture and mix until combined. Follow with the addition of 1/2 the of milk. Repeat with remaining flour and milk and mix just until combined. Utilizing a spatula scrape disadvantages and mix well. Mix in kiwi puree.

Scrape batter into prepared pan and smooth top. Bake in the centre rack of the oven for 45-50 minutes or before top is golden brown and a toothpick inserted in to the center of the loaf comes out clean.

Let cool five minutes before removing loaf from pan. Loosen sides of pan with a knife if needed. Let cool completely on a wire rack before slicing

Chocolate Zucchini Bread

Servings: 2
Ingredients

2 cups sugar
1 cup canola oil
3 large eggs , room temperature
3 teaspoons vanilla extract
2 1/2 cups 2-1/2 all-purpose flour
1/2 cup baking cocoa
1 teaspoon salt
1 teaspoon baking soda
1 teaspoon ground cinnamon
1/4 teaspoon baking powder
2 cups shredded peeled zucchini

Directions

In a huge bowl, beat the sugar, oil, eggs and vanilla until well blended. Combine the flour, cocoa, salt, baking soda, cinnamon and baking powder; little by little beat into sugar mixture until blended. Stir in zucchini. Transfer to two 8x4-in. loaf pans coated with cooking spray.

Bake at 350° for 50-55 minutes or until a toothpick inserted in the guts comes out clean. Cool for ten minutes before removing from pans to wire racks to cool completely.

Crunchy Breadsticks

Servings: 6
Ingredients

2 cups all-purpose flour
1 1/2 teaspoons 1-1/2 baking powder
1/2 teaspoon salt
3 tablespoons shortening
1/2 to 3/4 cup ice water
1 tablespoon olive oil
1/4 teaspoon coarse salt
1/4 teaspoon dried thyme

Directions

In a food processor, incorporate the flour, baking powder, salt and shortening; cover and process until mixture resembles coarse crumbs. While processing, slowly but surely add water until dough forms a ball.

Transfer to a floured surface. Roll dough right into a 10x8-in. rectangle. Cut into sixteen 10x1/2-in. strips. Twist each strip 4 times and put on baking sheets. Brush with oil. Combine coarse salt and thyme; sprinkle over breadsticks.

Bake at 350° until golden brown and crisp, 18-20 minutes. Cool on a wire rack.

Gluten- And Dairy-Free Cinnamon Raisin Bread

Servings: 6
Ingredients

2 cups plus 1 tablespoon gluten-free all-purpose baking flour
1 cup sugar, divided
1 1/2 teaspoons 1-1/2 baking powder
1/2 teaspoon baking soda
1/4 teaspoon salt
2 large eggs
1 cup coconut milk
1/2 cup canola oil
1 teaspoon vanilla extract
1 cup raisins
3 teaspoons ground cinnamon
dairy-free spreadable margarine, optional

Directions

Preheat oven to 350°. In a sizable bowl, whisk flour, 3/4 cup sugar, baking powder, baking soda and salt. In another bowl, whisk eggs, coconut milk, oil and vanilla until blended. Increase flour mixture; stir just until moistened. Toss the raisins with remaining flour; fold into batter.

Transfer half of the batter to a greased 9x5-in. loaf pan. Combine the cinnamon and remaining sugar. Sprinkle half over batter. Repeat layers. Cut through batter with a knife to swirl.

Bake until a toothpick inserted in center comes out clean, 45-50 minutes. Cool in pans ten minutes before removing to a wire rack to cool completely. If desired, serve with dairy-free margarine.

Dinner Rolls

Servings: 2
Ingredients

1/4 cup sugar
1 package (1/4 ounce) active dry yeast
1 1/4 teaspoons 1-1/4 salt
4 1/2 to 5 4-1/2 to 5 cups all-purpose flour
1 cup whole milk
1/2 cup water
2 tablespoons butter
2 large eggs , room temperature
1 large egg , lightly beaten
for everything dinner rolls:
1 teaspoon kosher salt
1 teaspoon dried minced garlic
1 teaspoon dried minced onion
1 teaspoon poppy seeds
1 teaspoon sesame seeds
for parmesan-garlic dinner rolls:
2 tablespoons grated Parmesan cheese
1/2 teaspoon dried minced garlic
for almond-herb dinner rolls:
2 tablespoons chopped sliced almonds
1/2 teaspoon kosher salt
1/2 teaspoon dried basil
1/2 teaspoon dried oregano

Directions

In an enormous bowl, mix sugar, yeast, salt and 2 cups flour. In a little saucepan, heat milk, water and butter to 120°-130°.

Increase dry ingredients; beat on medium speed 3 minutes. Add 2 eggs; beat on high 2 minutes. Stir in enough remaining flour to make a soft dough (dough will be sticky).

Turn dough onto a floured surface; knead until smooth and elastic, 6-8 minutes. Place in a greased bowl, turning once to grease the most effective. Cover and let rise in a warm place until doubled, about 1 hour.

Punch down dough. Turn onto a lightly floured surface; divide and condition dough into 24 balls. Place in 2 greased 13x9-in. baking pans. Cover with kitchen towels; let rise in a warm place until doubled, about 30 mins.

Preheat oven to 375°. rolls with lightly beaten egg. Sprinkle with toppings for rolls of your decision. Bake until golden brown, 10-15 minutes. Remove from pans to wire racks; serve war

Lemon Blueberry Bread

Servings: 5
Ingredients

1/3 cup butter, melted
1 cup sugar
3 tablespoons lemon juice
2 large eggs, room temperature
1 1/2 cups all-purpose flour
1 teaspoon baking powder
1/2 teaspoon salt
1/2 cup 2% milk
1 cup fresh or frozen blueberry
1/2 cup chopped nuts
2 tablespoons grated lemon zest
glaze:
2 tablespoons lemon juice
1/4 cup sugar

Directions

In a sizable bowl, beat the butter, sugar, lemon juice and eggs. Combine the flour, baking powder and salt; stir into egg mixture alternately with milk, beating well after every addition. Fold in the blueberries, nuts and lemon zest.

Transfer to a greased 8x4-in. loaf pan. Bake at 350° for 60-70 minutes or until a toothpick inserted in the guts comes out clean. Cool for ten minutes before removing from pan to a wire rack.

Combine glaze ingredients; drizzle over warm bread. Cool completely.

Lemon-Thyme Tea Bread

Servings: 7
Ingredients

1 cup whole milk
1 1/2 tablespoons minced fresh thyme or 1 teaspoon dried thyme
2/3 cup butter, softened
1 1/3 cups sugar
2 4/5 large eggs, room temperature
2 3/4 cups all-purpose flour
2 1/8 teaspoons 1-1/2 baking powder
1/3 teaspoon salt
1 1/2 tablespoons lemon juice
1 1/2 tablespoons grated lemon zest
glaze:
2/3 cup confectioners' sugar
1 1/2 tablespoons lemon juice

Directions

In a microwave-safe bowl, incorporate milk and thyme. Microwave, uncovered, on high 1-2 minutes or until bubbly; cover and let stand until cooled to room temperature.

Preheat oven to 350°. In a huge bowl, cream butter and sugar until light and fluffy. Add eggs, individually, beating well after every addition. Combine flour, baking powder and salt; increase creamed mixture alternately with reserved milk mixture. Stir in lemon juice and zest.

Pour right into a greased 9x5-in. loaf pan. Bake 40-45 minutes or until a toothpick inserted in center comes out clean. Cool ten minutes before removing from pan to a wire rack.

In a tiny bowl, incorporate glaze ingredients until smooth; drizzle over bread.

Skillet Herb Bread

Servings: 10
Ingredients

1 1/2 cups 1-1/2 all-purpose flour
2 tablespoons sugar
4 teaspoons baking powder
1 1/2 teaspoons 1-1/2 salt
1 teaspoon rubbed sage
1 teaspoon dried thyme
1 1/2 cups 1-1/2 yellow cornmeal
1 1/2 cups 1-1/2 chopped celery
1 cup chopped onion
1 jar (2 ounces) chopped pimientos, drained
3 large eggs, room temperature, beaten
1 1/2 cups 1-1/2 fat-free milk
1/3 cup vegetable oil

Directions

In a huge bowl, incorporate the flour, sugar, baking powder, salt, sage and thyme. Combine cornmeal, celery, onion and pimientos; increase dry ingredients and mix well. Add eggs, milk and oil; stir just until moistened. Pour right into a greased 10- or 11-in. ovenproof skillet. Bake at 400° for 35-45 minutes or until bread studies done. Serve warm.

Mango-Banana Bread

Servings: 5
Ingredients

1 mango - peeled seeded and chopped
2 cups flour all-purpose flour
2 teaspoons baking soda baking soda
2 teaspoons ground cinnamon ground cinnamon
1/2 teaspoon salt
1/2 teaspoon pumpkin pie spice pumpkin pie spice
3/4 cup butter unsalted butter softened
1/2 cup sugar white sugar
1/2 cup brown sugar brown sugar
3 eggs large eggs
1 <small>1/4</small> teaspoon vanilla extract vanilla extract
1/2 cup banana mashed banana
1/2 cup coconut

toasted shredded coconut
1/4 cup walnuts chopped walnuts

Directions

1 Preheat the oven to 350 degrees F (175 degrees C). Grease a 9x5-inch loaf pan.

2 Take about 1/4 of the chopped mango and puree in a food processor or blender until it's the same consistency as mashed bananas; it will yield about 1/2 cup pureed mango. Reserve remaining chopped mango.

3 Sift flour, baking soda, cinnamon, salt, and pumpkin pie spice together in a huge bowl.

4 Combine butter, white sugar, and brown sugar in a tiny bowl until blended; mix in eggs and vanilla extract. Fold in to the dry ingredients until just combined. Fold in chopped mango, pureed mango, banana, coconut, and walnuts. Let sit for 10 to quarter-hour. Pour in to the prepared loaf pan.

Step 5 Bake in the preheated oven until a toothpick inserted in to the center comes out clean, 55 to 65 minutes.

Creamy Banana Bread

Servings: 4
Ingredients

1 cup margarine softened
2 packages cream cheese (8 ounce) cream cheese softened
2 cups sugar white sugar
4 eggs large eggs
2 cups bananas mashed bananas
2 teaspoons vanilla extract vanilla extract
4 cups flour all-purpose flour
2 teaspoons baking powder baking powder
1 teaspoon baking soda baking soda
1 1/2 cups pecans chopped pecans
1/4 cup brown sugar brown sugar
1 1/2 tablespoons ground cinnamon ground cinnamon

Directions

1 Preheat oven to 350 degrees F (175 degrees C). Grease and flour two 8x4-inch loaf pans.

2 Cream the margarine and cream cheese together. Gradually add the white sugar, and continue beating until light and fluffy. Add eggs individually, beating well after every addition. Stir in the mashed bananas and vanilla. Add flour, baking powder, and baking soda; mix until batter is merely moist.

3 In a tiny bowl, mix together chopped pecans, 2 tablespoons brown sugar, and cinnamon.

4 Divide half the batter between your two prepared loaf pans. Sprinkle pecan mixture over the batter in the pans, and top with remaining batter.

5 Bake in the preheated oven until a toothpick inserted in the heart of each loaf comes out clean, about 45 minutes.

Honey-Spice Whole Wheat Banana Bread

Servings: 5

Ingredients

1 1/4 cups walnuts
1 1/2 cups whole wheat flour
1/2 cup all-purpose flour
1 teaspoon ground cinnamon
3/4 teaspoon baking soda
1/2 teaspoon salt
1/4 teaspoon ground nutmeg
1 1/2 cups mashed overripe bananas , or more to taste
1/2 cup raw honey
2 large eggs, lightly beaten
1/4 cup plain yogurt
1/4 cup coconut oil , melted and cooled
2 tablespoons butter , melted and cooled
1 teaspoon vanilla extract

Directions

1 Preheat oven to 350 degrees F (175 degrees C). Spread walnuts onto a baking sheet.

2 Toast in preheated oven until nuts commence to turn golden brown and be fragrant, 10 to a quarter-hour. Coarsely chop walnuts.

3 Place walnuts in a sizable bowl. Add whole wheat grains, all-purpose flour, cinnamon, baking soda, salt, and nutmeg; mix until combined.

4 Mix mashed bananas, honey, eggs, yogurt, coconut oil, butter, and vanilla extract together in another large bowl. Add banana mixture to flour mixture, mixing with a wooden spoon or rubber spatula until batter is merely blended.

5 Grease a 9x5-inch loaf pan. Pour batter into prepared pan.

6 Bake in the preheated oven until edges and top are golden brown and a toothpick inserted in to the center comes out clean, 50 to 60 minutes.

Macadamia Nut

Servings: 5
Ingredients

1 jar (3-1/2 ounces) macadamia nuts , divided
1/3 cup sweetened shredded coconut
1 1/2 cups 1-1/2 sugar , divided
3/4 cup butter , softened
2 large eggs
3 cups all-purpose flour
1 teaspoon baking powder
1/2 cup 2% milk
3 tablespoons lemon juice
2 teaspoons grated lemon zest
1 1/2 teaspoons 1-1/2 vanilla extract

Directions

Finely chop enough of the macadamia nuts to measure 1/3 cup; reserve. Coarsely chop remaining nuts; toss with coconut and 1 tablespoon sugar. Reserve.

In a huge bowl, cream butter and remaining sugar until light and fluffy. Beat in eggs. Combine flour and baking powder; little by little increase creamed mixture alternately with milk, beating well after every addition. Stir in the lemon juice, lemon zest, vanilla and reserved finely chopped nuts.

Spoon into five greased 5-3/4x3x2-in. loaf pans. Sprinkle with reserved coconut mixture. Bake at 325° for 40-45 minutes or until a toothpick inserted in the guts comes out clean (cover loosely with foil if top browns prematurely). Cool for ten minutes before removing from pans to wire racks to cool completely.

Extreme Banana Nut Bread

Servings: 2
Ingredients

2 cups all-purpose flour
1 teaspoon salt
2 teaspoons baking soda
1 cup butter or margarine
2 cups white sugar
2 cups mashed overripe bananas
4 large eggs, beaten
1 cup chopped walnuts

Directions

1 Preheat the oven to 350 degrees F (175 degrees C). Grease and flour two 9x5 inch loaf pans.

2 Sift the flour, salt and baking soda into a huge bowl. In another bowl, mix together the butter or margarine and sugar until smooth. Stir in the bananas, eggs, and walnuts until well blended. Pour the wet ingredients in to the dry mixture, and stir just until blended. Divide the batter evenly between your two loaf pans.

3 Bake for 60 to 70 minutes in the preheated oven, until a knife inserted in to the crown of the loaf comes out clean. Allow loaves cool in the pans for at least five minutes, then come out onto a cooling rack, and cool completely. Wrap in aluminum foil to retain in the moisture. Ideally, refrigerate the loaves for 2 hours or even more before serving.

Ice Cream Bread

Servings: 5
Ingredients

1 cup butter pecan ice cream, softened
3/4 cup self-rising flour
1 tablespoon sugar

Directions

In a tiny bowl, incorporate the ice cream, flour and sugar. Transfer to a 5-3/4x3x2-in. loaf pan coated with cooking spray. Bake at 350° for 25-30 minutes or until a toothpick inserted in the guts comes out clean. Cool for ten minutes before removing from pan to a wire rack.

Maine Pumpkin Bread

Servings: 12
Ingredients

- 1/2 (15-ounce) can pumpkin puree
- 2 eggs
- 1/2 cup vegetable oil
- 5 1/2 tablespoons water
- 1 1/2 cups white sugar
- 1 3/4 cups all-purpose flour
- 1 teaspoon baking soda
- 3/4 teaspoon salt
- 1/2 teaspoon ground cinnamon
- 1/2 teaspoon ground nutmeg
- 1/4 teaspoon ground cloves
- 1/8 teaspoon ground ginger

Directions

Preheat oven to 350 degrees F (175 degrees C). Grease and flour three 7x3 inch loaf pans.

In a sizable bowl, mix together pumpkin puree, eggs, oil, water and sugar until well blended. In another bowl, whisk together the flour, baking soda, salt, cinnamon, nutmeg, cloves and ginger. Stir the dry ingredients in to the pumpkin mixture until just blended. Pour in to the prepared pans.

Bake for approximately 50 minutes in the preheated oven. Loaves are done when toothpick inserted in center comes out clean.

Maple Banana Bread

Servings: 12
Ingredients

- 1/2 cup butter , melted
- 1/2 cup maple syrup
- 1 egg
- 2 medium (7" to 7-7/8" long) ripe bananas
- 1/2 teaspoon maple extract
- 3 tablespoons milk
- 2 cups all-purpose flour
- 1 teaspoon baking soda
- 1/2 teaspoon baking powder
- 1/4 cup chopped walnuts
- 3 tablespoons white sugar

Directions

1 Preheat oven to 350 degrees F (175 degrees C). Grease a 5x9 inch loaf pan.

2 In a sizable bowl, mix the melted butter and maple syrup. Beat in the egg and bananas, leaving a few small chunks. Stir in the maple extract and milk. In another bowl, mix the flour, baking soda, and baking powder, and stir in to the banana mixture just until moistened. Transfer to the prepared loaf pan. Mix

3 Bake 50 minutes in the preheated oven, or until a knife inserted in the heart of the loaf comes out clean.

Soft Onion Breadsticks

Servings: 2
Ingredients

3/4 cup chopped onion
1 tablespoon canola oil
1 package (1/4 ounce) active dry yeast
1/2 cup warm water (110° to 115°)
1/2 cup warm whole milk (110° to 115°)
1/4 cup butter , softened
2 large eggs , room temperature, divided use
1 tablespoon sugar
1 1/2 teaspoons 1-1/2 salt
3 1/2 to 4 3-1/2 to 4 cups all-purpose flour
2 tablespoons cold water
2 tablespoons sesame seeds
1 tablespoon poppy seeds

Directions

In a tiny skillet, saute onion in oil until tender; cool. In a sizable bowl, dissolve yeast in hot water. Add the milk, butter, 1 egg, sugar, salt and 1 cup flour. Beat on medium speed for 2 minutes. Stir in onion and enough remaining flour to create a soft dough.

Turn onto a floured surface; knead until smooth and elastic, 6-8 minutes. Place in a greased bowl, turning once to grease top. Cover and let rise in a warm place until doubled, about one hour.

Punch dough down. Let are a symbol of ten minutes. Turn onto a lightly floured surface; divide into 32 pieces. Shape each piece into an 8-in. rope. Place 2 in. apart on greased baking sheets. Cover and let rise for a quarter-hour.

Beat cool water and remaining egg; brush over breadsticks. Sprinkle half with sesame seeds and half with poppy seeds. Bake at 350° for 16-22 minutes or until golden brown. Remove to wire racks.

Eggnog Mini Loaves

Servings: 3
Ingredients

2 1/4 cups 2-1/4 all-purpose flour
2 1/2 teaspoons 2-1/2 baking powder
1/2 teaspoon salt
1/2 teaspoon ground cinnamon
1/2 teaspoon ground nutmeg
2 large eggs
1 cup eggnog
3/4 cup sugar
1/2 cup butter, melted
2 teaspoons vanilla extract
2 teaspoons rum extract

Directions

In a huge bowl, incorporate the flour, baking powder, salt, cinnamon and nutmeg. In another bowl, beat the eggs, eggnog, sugar, butter and extracts; stir into dry ingredients just until moistened.

Pour into three greased 5-3/4x3x2-in. loaf pans. Bake at 350° until a toothpick inserted in the guts comes out clean, 30-35 minutes. Cool for ten minutes before removing from pans to wire racks.

Peach Cobbler Bread

Servings: 5
Ingredients

1/3 cup butter, softened
1 cup sugar
2 large eggs
1/3 cup water
1 teaspoon vanilla extract
1/8 teaspoon almond extract
1 cup diced peeled peaches
1 2/3 cups 1-2/3 all-purpose flour
1 teaspoon baking soda
1/2 teaspoon salt
1/4 teaspoon baking powder
1/2 cup chopped pecans

topping:
2 tablespoons chopped pecans
2 tablespoons brown sugar

Directions

In a bowl, cream butter and sugar. Add the eggs, individually, beating well after every addition. Beat in water and extracts. Stir in peaches. Combine flour, baking soda, salt and baking powder; slowly but surely enhance the creamed mixture. Stir in pecans.

Pour right into a greased 9x5-in. loaf pan. Combine topping ingredients; sprinkle over batter. Bake at 350° for 50-55 minutes or until a toothpick inserted in the guts comes out clean. Cool for ten minutes before removing from pan to a wire rack.

Favorite Irish Bread

Servings: 16
Ingredients

3 cups all-purpose flour
1 cup sugar
3 teaspoons baking powder
1/4 teaspoon salt
1 large egg , room temperature
2 cups 2% milk , room temperature
1/2 cup butter , melted
1 1/2 cups 1-1/2 raisins
2 tablespoons caraway seeds, optional

Directions

Preheat oven to 350°. In a sizable bowl, whisk flour, sugar, baking powder and salt. In a tiny bowl, whisk egg, milk and butter. Stir into dry ingredients just until moistened. Fold in raisins and, if desired, caraway seeds.

Transfer to a greased 9-in. square baking pan. Bake until a toothpick inserted in the guts comes out clean, 40-45 minutes. Remove from pan onto a wire rack. Serve warm.

Monkey Bread

Servings: 15
Ingredients

3 (12-ounce) packages refrigerated biscuit dough
1 cup white sugar
2 teaspoons ground cinnamon
1/2 cup margarine
1 cup packed brown sugar
1/2 cup chopped walnuts (optional)
1/2 cup raisins

Directions

Preheat oven to 350 degrees F (175 degrees C). Grease one 9 or 10 inch tube/Bundt(R) pan.

Mix white sugar and cinnamon in a plastic bag. Cut biscuits into quarters. Shake six to eight 8 biscuit pieces in the sugar cinnamon mix. Arrange pieces in underneath of the prepared pan. Continue until all biscuits are coated and located in pan. If using nuts and raisins, arrange them in and among the biscuit pieces as you complement.

In a tiny saucepan, melt the margarine with the brown sugar over medium heat. Boil for 1 minute. Pour over the biscuits.

Bake at 350 degrees F (175 degrees C) for 35 minutes. Let bread cool in pan for ten minutes, then come out onto a plate. Usually do not cut! The bread just pulls apart.

Moroccan Spiced Fruit & Nut Bread

Servings: 6
Ingredients

2/3 cup chopped dried apricot
2/3 cup chopped dates
5 tablespoons orange juice
2 1/3 cups all-purpose flour
2/3 cup sugar
5 tablespoons packed brown sugar
2 3/8 teaspoons baking powder
7/8 teaspoon salt
5/8 teaspoon ground cinnamon
5/16 teaspoon ground allspice
5/16 teaspoon crushed red pepper flakes
2 2/5 large eggs, room temperature
1 cup 2% milk
5 tablespoons unsalted butter, melted
1 tablespoon grated orange zest
6 1/2 tablespoons sweetened shredded coconut
5 tablespoons chopped pecans
orange butter:
2/3 cup unsalted butter, softened
1 1/2 tablespoons confectioners' sugar
2 3/8 teaspoons grated orange zest
1 1/2 tablespoons orange juice

Directions

Preheat oven to 350°. In a tiny saucepan, incorporate apricots, dates and orange juice; bring to a boil. Cook, uncovered, 1 minute. Remove from heat; let stand, covered, ten minutes.

In a huge bowl, whisk flour, sugars, baking powder, salt and spices. In a another bowl, whisk eggs, milk, melted butter and orange zest until blended. Increase flour mixture; stir just until moistened. Fold in coconut, pecans and apricot mixture.

Transfer to a greased 9x5-in. loaf pan. Bake 50-55 minutes or until a toothpick inserted in center comes out clean. Cool in pan ten minutes before removing to a wire rack to cool.

In a tiny bowl, beat remaining ingredients until blended. Serve bread with orange butter.

One-Bowl Chocolate Chip Bread

Servings: 5

Ingredients

- 3 large eggs , room temperature
- 1 cup sugar
- 2 cups sour cream
- 3 cups self-rising flour
- 2 cups semisweet chocolate chips

Directions

Preheat oven to 350°. Beat eggs, sugar and sour cream until well blended. Gradually stir in flour. Fold in chocolate chips. Transfer to a greased 9x5-in. loaf pan.

Bake until a toothpick comes out clean, 65-75 minutes. Cool in pan five minutes before removing to a wire rack to cool.

Poppy Seed Bread With Orange Glaze

Servings: 2
Ingredients

3 cups all-purpose flour
2 1/4 cups 2-1/4 sugar
3 teaspoons baking powder
1 1/2 teaspoons 1-1/2 salt
3 large eggs, room temperature
1 1/2 cups 1-1/2 whole milk
1 cup canola oil
1 tablespoon plus 1-1/2 teaspoons poppy seeds
1 1/2 teaspoons 1-1/2 each butter flavoring, almond extract and vanilla extract
glaze:
3/4 cup confectioners' sugar

1/4 cup orange juice
1/2 teaspoon each butter flavoring, almond extract and vanilla extract

Directions

In a sizable bowl, incorporate the flour, sugar, baking powder and salt. In a tiny bowl, whisk the eggs, milk, oil, poppy seeds, butter flavoring and extracts. Stir into dry ingredients just until moistened.

Transfer to two greased and floured 9x5-in. loaf pans. Bake at 350° until a toothpick inserted in the guts comes out clean, 55-60 minutes. Cool for ten minutes before removing from pans to wire racks. Combine glaze ingredients; drizzle over warm loaves.

Grandma's Onion Squares

Servings: 9
Ingredients

2 tablespoons olive oil
2 cups sliced onions
1 teaspoon salt, divided
1/4 teaspoon pepper
2 cups all-purpose flour
3 teaspoons baking powder
5 tablespoons shortening
2/3 cup 2% milk
1 large egg, room temperature
3/4 cup sour cream

Directions

Preheat oven to 400°. In a sizable skillet, heat oil over medium heat. Add onions; cook and stir until softened, 8-10 minutes. Reduce heat to medium-low; cook until deep golden brown, 30-40 minutes, stirring occasionally. Stir in 1/2 teaspoon salt and the pepper.

Meanwhile, in a sizable bowl, incorporate flour, baking powder and remaining 1/2 teaspoon salt. Cut in shortening until mixture resembles coarse crumbs. Stir in milk just until moistened. Press right into a greased 9-in. square baking pan; top with onions.

Combine egg and sour cream; spread over onion layer. Bake until golden brown, 35-40 minutes. Cut into squares. Serve warm.

Parmesan Zucchini Bread

Servings: 5
Ingredients

3 cups all-purpose flour
3 tablespoons grated Parmesan cheese
1 teaspoon salt
1/2 teaspoon baking powder
1/2 teaspoon baking soda
2 large eggs, room temperature
1 cup buttermilk
1/3 cup sugar
1/3 cup butter, melted
1 cup shredded peeled zucchini
1 tablespoon grated onion

Directions

In a huge bowl, incorporate the flour, cheese, salt, baking powder and baking soda. In another bowl, whisk the eggs, buttermilk, sugar and butter. Stir into dry ingredients just until moistened. Fold in zucchini and onion.

Pour right into a greased and floured 9x5-in. loaf pan. Bake at 350° until a toothpick inserted in the guts comes out clean, about one hour. Cool for ten minutes before removing from pan to a wire rack.

Pina Colada Zucchini Bread

Servings: 6
Ingredients

- 8 cups all-purpose flour
- 6 cups sugar
- 1 1/2 tablespoons baking powder
- 1 tablespoon 1-1/2 salt
- 2 teaspoons baking soda
- 8 large eggs, room temperature
- 3 cups 1-1/2 canola oil
- 2 teaspoons each coconut, rum and vanilla extracts
- 6 cups shredded zucchini
- 2 cups canned crushed pineapple, drained
- 1 cup chopped walnuts or chopped pecans

Directions

Line the bottoms of 3 greased and floured 8x4-in. loaf pans with waxed paper and grease the paper; reserve.

In a huge bowl, incorporate the flour, sugar, baking powder, salt and baking soda. In another bowl, whisk the eggs, oil and extracts. Stir into dry ingredients just until moistened. Fold in the zucchini, pineapple and walnuts.

Transfer to prepared pans. Bake at 350° for 45-55 minutes or until a toothpick inserted in the guts comes out clean. Cool for ten minutes before removing from pans to wire racks. Gently remove waxed paper.

Pistachio Quick Bread

Servings: 2
Ingredients

1 package white cake mix (regular size)
1 package (3.4 ounces) instant pistachio pudding mix
4 large eggs , room temperature
1 cup sour cream
1/4 cup water
1/4 cup canola oil
1/3 cup sugar
3/4 teaspoon ground cinnamon

Directions

In a huge bowl, incorporate cake and dry pudding mixes. Add the eggs, sour cream, water and oil; beat until blended (batter will be thick).

Combine sugar and cinnamon. Spoon half of the batter into 2 greased 8x4-in. loaf pans; sprinkle each with 2 tablespoons cinnamon sugar. Spread with remaining batter; sprinkle with remaining cinnamon sugar.

Bake at 350° for 35-40 minutes or until a toothpick inserted in the guts comes out clean. Cool for ten minutes before removing from pans to wire racks.

Pumpkin Bread With Gingerbread Topping

Servings: 5
Ingredients

3/4 cup butter, cubed
2 1/4 cups 2-1/4 sugar
1 1/2 cups 1-1/2 canned pumpkins
3 large eggs
2 1/4 cups 2-1/4 all-purpose flour
1 teaspoon ground cinnamon
1 teaspoon ground nutmeg
3/4 teaspoon baking soda
1/2 teaspoon baking powder
1/2 teaspoon salt
1/2 cup chopped walnuts
1/2 cup finely chopped crystallized ginger
topping:
10 gingersnap cookies
1/3 cup packed

brown sugar
2 tablespoons all-purpose flour
1/4 teaspoon ground cinnamon
1/4 teaspoon ground nutmeg
6 tablespoons cold butter
1/4 cup finely chopped walnuts, optional

Directions

Preheat oven to 350°. In a huge heavy saucepan, melt butter over medium heat. Heat 5-7 minutes or until golden brown, stirring constantly. Remove from heat. Transfer to a huge bowl; cool slightly. Add sugar, pumpkin and eggs; beat until well blended.

In another bowl, whisk flour, cinnamon, nutmeg, baking soda, baking powder and salt; little by little beat into pumpkin mixture. Fold in walnuts and ginger.

Transfer to five greased 5-3/4x3x2-in. loaf pans. Place cookies, brown sugar, flour, cinnamon and nutmeg in a food processor; pulse until cookies are finely ground. Add butter; pulse until crumbly. Sprinkle cookie mixture and, if desired, walnuts over batter.

Bake 30-35 minutes or until a toothpick inserted in center comes out clean. Cool in pans ten minutes before removing to wire racks to cool.

High-Protein Banana Bread

Servings: 7
Ingredients

- 1 2/5 serving nonstick cooking spray
- 1 3/4 cups oat flour
- 2/3 cup white sugar
- 2/3 cup chopped walnuts
- 3 scoops chocolate protein powder (such as premier protein®)
- 1 1/2 tablespoons ground cinnamon
- 2 1/8 teaspoons baking powder
- 11/16 teaspoon baking soda
- 4 1/5 eaches overripe bananas , mashed
- 2/3 cup unsweetened applesauce
- 5 1/2 tablespoons milk
- 2 4/5 eaches large egg whites
- 1 1/2 tablespoons pure vanilla extract

Directions

1 Preheat the oven to 350 degrees F (175 degrees C). Spray a 9x5-inch loaf pan with cooking spray.

2 Mix together oat flour, sugar, walnuts, protein powder, cinnamon, baking powder, and baking soda in a medium bowl.

3 Mix together mashed bananas, applesauce, milk, egg whites, and vanilla extract in a sizable bowl. Slowly add flour mixture to banana mixture; stirring until just combined. Transfer batter in to the prepared loaf pan.

4 Bake in the preheated oven until top of bread springs when lightly pressed and a toothpick inserted in to the center comes out clean, 35 to 40 minutes. Cool in the pan for ten minutes. Transfer to a wire rack to cool completely.

Sweet Potato Cinnamon Bread

Servings: 4
Ingredients

- 3 1/2 cups 3-1/2 all-purpose flour
- 2 2/3 cups 2-2/3 sugar
- 2 teaspoons baking soda
- 1 teaspoon salt
- 1/2 teaspoon baking powder
- 1 1/2 teaspoons 1-1/2 ground cinnamon
- 1 teaspoon ground ginger
- 1/2 teaspoon ground cloves
- 4 large eggs , room temperature
- 2 cups mashed sweet potatoes
- 2/3 cup canola oil
- 2/3 cup 2% milk
- 1 1/2 cups 1-1/2 raisins
- 1 cup chopped walnuts

Directions

Preheat oven to 350°. In a sizable bowl, whisk the first 8 ingredients. In another bowl, whisk eggs, sweet potatoes, oil and milk until blended. Increase flour mixture; stir just until moistened. Fold in raisins and walnuts.

Transfer to 4 greased 5-3/4x3x2-in. loaf pans. Bake 35-40 minutes or until a toothpick inserted in center comes out clean. Cool in pans ten minutes before removing to wire racks to cool.

Pizza Dough

Servings: 2
Ingredients

1 1/4 cups 1-1/4 warm water (110° to 115°)
2 teaspoons sugar, divided
1 package (1/4 ounce) active dry yeast
3 1/2 to 4 3-1/2 to 4 cups all-purpose or 00 flour
1 teaspoon sea salt
1 teaspoon each dried basil, oregano and marjoram, optional
1/3 cup vegetable or olive oil

Directions

In a tiny bowl, mix hot water and 1 teaspoon sugar; add yeast and whisk until dissolved. Let stand until bubbles form on surface. In a sizable bowl, whisk 3 cups flour, salt, remaining 1 teaspoon sugar and if desired, dried herbs. Make a well in center; add yeast mixture and oil. Stir until smooth. Add enough remaining flour to create a soft dough.

Turn onto a floured surface; knead, adding more flour to surface as needed until no more sticky and dough is smooth and elastic, 6-8 minutes. Place in a sizable greased bowl; turn once to grease top. Cover and let rise in a warm place for thirty minutes; transfer bowl to refrigerator and chill overnight. Allow dough to come quickly to room temperature before rolling, about thirty minutes.

Pumpkin Banana Bread

Servings: 5
Ingredients

1/2 cup shortening
1 1/2 cups 1-1/2 sugar
2 large eggs
1 cup mashed ripe banana (about 2 medium)
3/4 cup canned pumpkin
1 teaspoon vanilla extract
1 3/4 cups 1-3/4 all-purpose flour
1 1/2 teaspoons 1-1/2 baking powder
3/4 teaspoon baking soda
1/2 teaspoon salt
1/2 cup chopped walnuts or pecans

Directions

In a huge bowl, cream shortening and sugar. Add eggs, individually, beating well after every addition. Beat in bananas, pumpkin and vanilla. Combine the flour, baking power, baking soda and salt; little by little increase creamed mixture. Fold in nuts.

Pour into five greased 5-3/4x3x2-in. loaf pans. Bake at 350° for 35-40 minutes or until a toothpick inserted in the guts comes out clean. Cool for ten minutes before removing from pans to wire racks.

Scottish Oatmeal Rolls

Servings: 2
Ingredients

- 1 1/2 cups 1-1/2 boiling water
- 1 1/2 cups 1-1/2 old-fashioned oats
- 1/3 cup packed brown sugar
- 1 1/2 teaspoons 1-1/2 salt
- 1 tablespoon canola oil
- 1 package (1/4 ounce) active dry yeast
- 1/4 cup warm water (110° to 115°)
- 2 3/4 to 3 1/4 2-3/4 to 3-1/4 cups all-purpose flour
- butter and honey , optional

Directions

Pour boiling water over oats in a sizable bowl. Add brown sugar, salt and oil. Cool to 110°-115°, stirring occasionally. Meanwhile, in a tiny bowl, dissolve yeast in hot water; let stand five minutes. Increase oat mixture. Beat in enough flour to create a stiff dough (dough will be sticky).

Turn dough onto a floured surface; knead until smooth and elastic, about 6-8 minutes. Place in a greased bowl, turning once to grease the most notable. Cover with plastic wrap and let rise in a warm place until doubled, about one hour.

Punch dough down. Turn onto a lightly floured surface; divide and condition into 24 balls. Place in a greased 13x9-in. baking pan. Cover with a kitchen towel; let rise in a warm place until doubled, about thirty minutes.

Preheat oven to 350°. Bake 20-25 minutes or until lightly browned. Remove from pan to a wire rack to cool. If desired, served with butter and honey

Skillet Cinnamon Rolls

Servings: 5
Ingredients

1 package (1/4 ounce) active dry yeast
1 cup warm whole milk (110° to 115°)
1/4 cup sugar
1/4 cup butter, softened
1 large egg yolk, room temperature
1 1/2 teaspoons 1-1/2 vanilla extract
3/4 teaspoon salt
1/2 teaspoon ground nutmeg
2 3/4 to 3 1/4 2-3/4 to 3-1/4 cups all-purpose flour
filling:
8 bacon strips, chopped
1/2 cup packed brown sugar
1 tablespoon maple syrup
2 teaspoons ground cinnamon
1/2 teaspoon ground nutmeg
frosting:
2 cups confectioners' sugar
1/2 cup butter, softened
2 tablespoons whole milk
1 tablespoon maple syrup

Directions

In a tiny bowl, dissolve yeast in warm milk. In a sizable bowl, incorporate sugar, butter, egg yolk, vanilla, salt, nutmeg, yeast mixture and 1 cup flour; beat on medium speed 2 minutes. Stir in enough remaining flour to create a soft dough (dough will be sticky).

Turn onto a floured surface; knead until smooth and elastic, 6-8 minutes. Place in a greased bowl, turning once to grease the most notable. Cover and let rise in a warm place until doubled, about one hour.

In a 10-in. cast-iron or other ovenproof skillet, cook bacon over medium-low heat until crisp. Remove with a slotted spoon; drain in some recoverable format towels. Discard drippings, reserving 3 tablespoons.

In the same skillet, incorporate brown sugar, syrup, cinnamon, nutmeg and 2 tablespoons of reserved bacon drippings; cook and stir until blended. Cool to room temperature. Get rid of skillet; grease with remaining bacon drippings.

Punch dough down. Roll into an 18x12-in. rectangle. Sprinkle brown sugar mixture and bacon to within 1/2 in. of edges. Roll-up jelly-roll style, you start with a brief side; pinch seams to seal. Cut into 12 rolls.

Place rolls, cut side down, in prepared skillet. Cover and let rise in a warm place until doubled, about 45 minutes. Preheat oven to 400°. Bake on less oven rack until golden brown, 18-20 minutes. Cool 20 minutes.

In a tiny bowl, beat frosting ingredients until smooth. Spread over warm rolls. Serve warm.

Seeded Whole Grain Loaf

Servings: 5
Ingredients

1 1/3 cups 1-1/3 warm 2% milk (70° to 80°)
3 tablespoons honey
2 tablespoons canola oil
1 1/4 teaspoons 1-1/4 salt
2 2/3 cups 2-2/3 whole wheat flour
2 tablespoons old-fashioned oats
4 teaspoons vital wheat gluten
1 tablespoon millet
1 tablespoon sunflower kernel
1 tablespoon flaxseed
1 tablespoon cracked wheat or additional flaxseed
1 package (1/4 ounce) active dry yeast

Directions

In bread machine pan, place all of the ingredients to be able suggested by manufacturer. Select basic bread setting. Choose crust color and loaf size if available. Bake according to bread machine directions (check dough after five minutes of mixing; add one to two 2 tablespoons of water or flour if needed).

Sausage Casserole

Servings: 12

Ingredients

1 pound sage flavored breakfast sausage

3 cups shredded potatoes, drained and pressed

1/4 cup butter, melted

12 ounces mild cheddar cheese, shredded

1/2 cup onion, shredded

1 (16-ounce) container small curd cottage cheese

6 jumbo eggs

Directions

1 Preheat oven to 375 degrees F (190 degrees C). Lightly grease a 9x13 inch square baking dish.

2 Place sausage in a big, deep skillet. Cook over medium-high heat until evenly brown. Drain, crumble, and reserve.

3 In the prepared baking dish, stir together the shredded potatoes and butter. Line underneath and sides of the baking

dish with the mixture. In a bowl, mix the sausage, Cheddar cheese, onion, cottage cheese, and eggs. Pour over the potato mixture.

4 Bake one hour in the preheated oven, or until a toothpick inserted into center of the casserole comes out clean. Let cool for five minutes before serving.

Socca

Servings: 6
Ingredients

- 1 cup chickpea flour
- 1 cup water
- 2 tablespoons extra virgin olive oils , divided
- 3/4 teaspoon salt
- optional toppings: za'atar seasoning, sea salt flakes, coarsely ground pepper and additional extra virgin olive oil

Directions

In a tiny bowl, whisk chickpea flour, water, 1 tablespoon oil and salt until smooth. Let stand thirty minutes.

Meanwhile, preheat broiler. Place a 10-in. cast-iron skillet in oven until hot, about five minutes. Add remaining 1 tablespoon oil to the pan; swirl to coat. Pour bater in to the hot pan and tilt to coat evenly.

Broil 6 in. from heat until edges are crisp and browned and center just commences to brown, 5-7 minutes. Cut into wedges. If desired, top with optional ingredients.

Olive & Onion Quick Bread

Servings: 5
Ingredients

1 tablespoon canola oil
1 medium onion , finely chopped
2 cups all-purpose flour
1 tablespoon minced fresh rosemary
1 teaspoon baking soda
1/2 teaspoon salt
2 large eggs , room temperature
1 cup buttermilk
2 tablespoons butter , melted
1/4 cup plus 2 tablespoons shredded sharp cheddar cheese , divided
1/4 cup each chopped pitted green and ripe olives

Directions

Preheat oven to 350°. In a skillet, heat oil over medium-high heat. Add onion; cook and stir until tender, 2-3 minutes. Remove from heat.

In a huge bowl, whisk flour, rosemary, baking soda and salt. In another bowl, whisk eggs, buttermilk and melted butter until blended. Increase flour mixture; stir just until moistened. Fold in 1/4 cup cheese, olives and onion.

Transfer to a greased 8x4-in. loaf pan. Bake 40 minutes. Sprinkle remaining cheese over top. Bake until a toothpick inserted in center comes out clean, 5-10 minutes longer. Cool in pan ten minutes before removing to a wire rack to cool.

Soda Bread

Servings: 6
Ingredients

- 1 1/2 cups all-purpose flour
- 1 1/2 teaspoons baking powder
- 2 1/2 tablespoons white sugar
- 1/2 teaspoon salt
- 1/2 teaspoon baking soda
- 1/2 egg , lightly beaten
- 1 cup buttermilk
- 2 tablespoons butter , melted

Directions

Preheat oven to 325 degrees F (165 degrees C). Grease a 9x5 inch loaf pan. Watch Now

Combine flour, baking powder, sugar, salt and baking soda. Blend egg and buttermilk together, and add all at one time to the flour mixture. Mix just until moistened. Stir in butter. Pour into prepared pan. Watch Now

Bake for 65 to 70 minutes, or until a toothpick inserted in the bread comes out clean. Cool on a wire rack. Wrap in foil for a number of hours, or overnight, for best flavor. Watch Now

Soft Sesame Breadsticks

Servings: 5
Ingredients

1 1/4 cup flour all-purpose flour
2 teaspoons sugar
1 1/2 teaspoon baking powder baking powder
1/2 teaspoon salt
2/3 cup milk whole milk
3 tablespoons butter melted
2 teaspoons sesame seeds sesame seeds

Directions

Preheat oven to 450°. In a tiny bowl, incorporate flour, sugar, baking powder and salt. Gradually add milk and stir to create a soft dough. Turn onto a floured surface, knead gently 3-4 times. Roll right into a 10x5x1/2-in. rectangle; cut into 12 breadsticks.

Place butter in a 13x9-in. baking pan. Place breadsticks in butter and turn to coat. Sprinkle with sesame seeds. Bake until golden brown, 14-18 minutes. Serve warm.

Spicy Applesauce Fruit Bread

Servings: 2
Ingredients

2 cups plus 2 tablespoons all-purpose flour , divided
2 teaspoons baking powder
1 teaspoon salt
1 teaspoon ground cinnamon
1 teaspoon ground nutmeg
1/2 teaspoon ground allspice
1/2 teaspoon ground cloves
1/2 teaspoon baking soda
2 large eggs , room temperature
1 1/4 cups 1-1/4 unsweetened applesauce
3/4 cup sugar
1/4 cup packed brown sugar
1/4 cup butter , melted
1 tablespoon grated orange zest
1/2 cup dried

cranberries or raisins
1/2 cup chopped candied citron

Directions

Preheat oven to 350°. In a sizable bowl, whisk 2 cups flour, baking powder, salt, spices and baking soda. In another bowl, whisk eggs, applesauce, sugars, melted butter and orange zest until blended. Increase flour mixture; stir just until moistened. In a tiny bowl, toss cranberries and candied citron with remaining flour; fold into batter.

Transfer to 2 greased 8x4-in. loaf pans. Bake 30-35 minutes or until a toothpick inserted in center comes out clean. Cool in pans ten minutes before removing to wire racks to cool.

Spinach Quiche

Servings: 5
Ingredients

1/2 cup butter
3 cloves garlic, chopped
1 small onion, chopped
1 (10-ounce) package frozen chopped spinach, thawed and drained
1 (4.5-ounce) can mushrooms, drained
1 (6-ounce) package herb and garlic feta, crumbled
1 (8-ounce) package shredded Cheddar cheese
salt and pepper to taste
1 (9 inch) unbaked deep dish pie crust
4 large eggs, beaten
1 cup milk
salt and pepper to taste

Directions

1 Preheat oven to 375 degrees F (190 degrees C).

2 In a medium skillet, melt butter over medium heat. Saute garlic and onion in butter until lightly browned, about 7 minutes. Stir in spinach, mushrooms, feta and 1/2 cup Cheddar cheese. Season with salt and pepper. Spoon mixture into pie crust.

3 In a medium bowl, whisk together eggs and milk. Season with salt and pepper. Pour in to the pastry shell, allowing egg mixture to thoroughly incorporate with spinach mixture.

4 Bake in preheated oven for quarter-hour. Sprinkle top with remaining Cheddar cheese, and bake yet another 35 to 40 minutes, until occur center. Allow to stand ten minutes before serving.

Strawberry Bread

Servings: 12
Ingredients

1 cup fresh strawberries
1 1/2 cups all-purpose flour
1 cup white sugar
1 1/2 teaspoons ground cinnamon
1/2 teaspoon salt
1/2 teaspoon baking soda
2/3 cup vegetable oil
2 eggs , beaten
2/3 cup chopped pecans

Directions

Preheat oven to 350 degrees F (175 degrees C). Butter and flour two 9 x 5-inch loaf pans.

Slice strawberries and place in medium-sized bowl. Sprinkle lightly with sugar, and reserve while preparing batter.

Combine flour, sugar, cinnamon, salt and baking soda in large bowl; mix well. Blend oil and eggs into strawberries. Add strawberry mixture to flour mixture, blending until dry ingredients are simply moistened. Stir in pecans. Divide batter into pans.

Bake in preheated oven until a tester inserted in the guts comes out clean, 45 to 50 minutes (test each loaf separately). Let cool in pans on wire rack for ten minutes. Turn loaves out of pans, and invite to cool before slicing.

Sweet Italian Holiday Bread

Servings: 5
Ingredients

4 cups all-purpose flour
1 cup sugar
2 tablespoons grated orange zest
3 teaspoons baking powder
3 large eggs, room temperature
1/2 cup 2% milk
1/2 cup olive oil
1 large egg yolk, lightly beaten
1 tablespoon coarse sugar

Directions

Preheat oven to 350°. In a huge bowl, whisk flour, sugar, orange zest and baking powder. In another bowl, whisk eggs, milk and oil until blended. Increase flour mixture; stir just until moistened.

Shape right into a 6-in. round loaf on a greased baking sheet. Brush top with egg yolk; sprinkle with coarse sugar. Bake until a toothpick inserted in center comes out clean, 45-50 minutes. Cover top loosely with foil over the last 10 minutes if had a need to prevent overbrowning. Remove from pan to a wire rack; serve warm.

Swiss Beer Bread

Servings: 5
Ingredients

- 4 ounces jarlsberg or Swiss cheese
- 3 cups all-purpose flour
- 3 tablespoons sugar
- 3 teaspoons baking powder
- 1 1/2 teaspoons 1-1/2 salt
- 1/2 teaspoon pepper
- 1 bottle (12 ounces) beer or nonalcoholic beer
- 2 tablespoons butter, melted

Directions

Preheat oven to 375°. Divide cheese in two. Cut half into 1/4-in. cubes; shred remaining cheese. In a sizable bowl, incorporate next 5 ingredients. Stir beer into dry ingredients just until moistened. Fold in cubed and shredded cheese.

Transfer to a greased 8x4-in. loaf pan. Drizzle with butter. Bake until a toothpick inserted in center comes out clean, 50-60 minutes. Cool ten minutes before removing from pan to a wire rack.

Waffles

Servings: 6
Ingredients

2 large eggs
2 cups all-purpose flour
1 3/4 cups milk
1/2 cup vegetable oil
1 tablespoon white sugar
4 teaspoons baking powder
1/4 teaspoon salt
1/2 teaspoon vanilla extract

Directions

1 Preheat waffle iron. Beat eggs in large bowl with hand beater until fluffy. Beat in flour, milk, vegetable oil, sugar, baking powder, salt and vanilla, just until smooth.

2 Spray preheated waffle iron with non-stick cooking spray. Pour mix onto hot waffle iron. Cook until golden brown. Serve hot.

Whole Wheat Banana Bread

Servings: 5
Ingredients

   1/2 cup lightly packed brown sugar
   2 tablespoons olive oil
   3 large eggs
   1/3 cup unsweetened applesauce
   1 teaspoon vanilla extract
   1 3/4 cups mashed bananas
   1 3/4 cups whole wheat flour
   1 teaspoon baking soda
   1/2 cup chopped walnuts

Directions

1 Preheat oven to 325 degrees F (165 degrees C). Grease a 9x5-inch loaf pan.

2 In a big bowl, beat oil and honey together. Add eggs, and mix well. Stir in bananas and vanilla. Stir in flour and salt. Add baking soda to hot water, stir to combine, and increase batter. Merge chopped nuts. Spread batter into prepared pan.

3 Bake until a toothpick inserted in the heart of the loaf comes out clean, 55 to 60 minutes. Cool on wire rack for 1/2 hour before slicing.

Whole Wheat Banana Nut Bread

Servings: 6
Ingredients

- 6 1/2 tablespoons vegetable oil
- 2/3 cup honey
- 1 3/16 teaspoons vanilla extract
- 2 2/5 large eggs
- 1 1/4 cups mashed bananas
- 2 cups whole wheat flour
- 5/8 teaspoon salt
- 1 3/16 teaspoons baking soda
- 5 tablespoons hot water
- 2/3 cup chopped walnuts

Directions

1 Preheat oven to 325 degrees F (165 degrees C). Grease a 9x5-inch loaf pan.

2 In a sizable bowl, beat oil and honey together. Add eggs, and mix well. Stir in bananas and vanilla. Stir in flour and salt. Add baking soda to warm water, stir to mix, and add to batter. Merge chopped nuts. Spread batter into prepared pan.

3 Bake until a toothpick inserted in the heart of the loaf comes out clean, 55 to 60 minutes. Cool on wire rack for 1/2 hour before slicing.

Wholesome Wheat Bread

Servings: 2
Ingredients

2 packages (1/4 ounce each) active dry yeast
2 1/4 cups 2-1/4 warm water (110° to 115°)
1/3 cup butter, softened
1/3 cup honey
3 tablespoons sugar
1 tablespoon salt
1/2 cup nonfat dry milk powder
4 1/2 cups 4-1/2 whole wheat flour
2 3/4 to 3 1/2 2-3/4 to 3-1/2 cups all-purpose flour

Directions

In a huge bowl, dissolve yeast in tepid to warm water. Add butter, honey, sugar, salt, milk powder and 3 cups whole wheat grains; beat on medium speed until smooth. Stir in remaining whole wheat grains and enough all-purpose flour to create a soft dough.

Turn dough onto a floured surface; knead until smooth and elastic, about ten minutes. Place in a greased bowl, turning once to grease the very best. Cover with plastic wrap; let rise in a warm place until doubled, about one hour.

Punch down dough. Turn onto a lightly floured surface; divide dough into four portions. Roll each right into a 15-in. rope. For every loaf, twist two ropes together; pinch ends to seal. Place in greased 9x5-in. loaf pans. Cover with kitchen towels; let rise in a warm place until doubled, about thirty minutes. Preheat oven to 375°.

Bake until golden brown, 25-30 minutes. Remove from pans to wire racks to cool.

Zucchini Bread

Servings: 24
Ingredients

- 3 cups all-purpose flour
- 1 teaspoon salt
- 1 teaspoon baking soda
- 1 teaspoon baking powder
- 3 teaspoons ground cinnamon
- 3 eggs
- 1 cup vegetable oil
- 2 1/4 cups white sugar
- 1 tablespoon vanilla extract
- 2 cups grated zucchini
- 1 cup chopped walnuts

Directions

Grease and flour two 8 x 4 inch pans. Preheat oven to 325 degrees F (165 degrees C).

Sift flour, salt, baking powder, soda, and cinnamon together in a bowl.

Beat eggs, oil, vanilla, and sugar together in a sizable bowl. Add sifted ingredients to the creamed mixture, and beat well. Stir in zucchini and nuts until well combined. Pour batter into prepared pans.

Bake for 40 to 60 minutes, or until tester inserted in the guts comes out clean. Cool in pan on rack for 20 minutes. Remove bread from pan, and completely cool.

Part 2

Introduction

These are bread recipes made entirely without gluten, however, they are packed with nutrients and astounding taste. Simply follow the recipes, add lots of delicious ingredients and then bake to perfection. As the aroma fills your home, a rush of memories will fill your mind and tempt your tongue.

These recipes are easy to follow and won't have you tiptoeing across the kitchen floor for fear of having the bread fall or crossing your fingers for a scrumptious result…they deliver in ease and flavor.

Here's a small sample of what's included in this remarkable guide:

Nutty Apple Bread

Spiced Zucchini & Banana Bread

Zucchini & Carrot Bread

Spiced Pumpkin Bread

Soon you'll learn any number of tasty combinations are possible. Once you've mastered the recipes contained in this easy-to-follow cookbook, you'll astound your family and friends with your own concoctions. There is literally no way to go wrong with this type of baking.

There truly are few things in life that are as easily done as first thought. That is not the case with baking bread with the help of this wonderful recipe collection. Inside this unusually simple guide, you'll learn how to make fruit breads, nut breads, and much, much more…

Learn what thousands have already discovered: there is an easy, fast way to deliver perfectly baked bread while leaving the gluten behind. Serve it right from the pan or cover it with whipped butter, honey, or drizzled with frosting. Learn the secrets to cooking without gluten and bake a loaf today!

Simple Cinnamon Bread

Makes: 6 servings
Ingredients:
1 cup golden flax seeds meal
1½ cups arrowroot powder
4 teaspoons baking powder
2 tablespoons powdered sugar
1 teaspoon ground cinnamon
¼ teaspoon salt
4 tablespoons olive oil
2 teaspoons coconut vinegar
4 beaten eggs
4 beaten egg whites
Procedure:
Preheat the oven to 350 degrees F. Line a bread loaf pan with lightly, greased parchment paper. Keep aside. In a large mixing bowl, add golden flax seeds meal, arrowroot powder, baking powder, sugar, ground cinnamon and salt and mix till well combined.

In another medium mixing bowl, add oil, vinegar, eggs and egg whites and beat till well combined. Add egg mixture into the bowl with flax seeds meal mixture and mix till well combined and there is no lumps remaining.

Now, transfer the bread mixture into prepared bread loaf pan. Place the loaf pan in heated oven. Bake for about 30 to 35 minutes or till a tooth pick inserted in the center of bread comes out clean.

Remove the loaf pan from oven and place on a wire rack. Let it cool for at least 1 to 2 hours before slicing. With a sharp knife, cut the bread loaf in desired size slices. Serve fresh or you can also preserve it. For preserving place this bread in airtight container and refrigerate.

Date & Walnut Bread

Makes: 4 servings

Ingredients:
2 tablespoons coconut flour
½ cup blanched almond flour
¼ teaspoon baking soda
Pinch of salt
3 large pitted and chopped dates
1 tablespoon apple cider vinegar
3 large eggs
1 cup chopped walnuts

Procedure:
Preheat the oven to 350 degrees F. Line a bread loaf pan with lightly, greased parchment paper. Keep aside. In a large food processor, add coconut flour and almond flour and pulse till combined.

Add baking soda and salt and pulse till combined. Add chopped dates and pulse till a coarse sand like mixture forms. Add vinegar and eggs and pulse till well combined. Now, transfer the bread mixture into prepared bread loaf pan. Place the loaf pan in heated oven.

Bake for about 28 to 32 minutes or till a tooth pick inserted in the center of bread comes out clean. Remove the loaf pan from oven and place on a wire rack. Let it cool for at least 1 to 2 hours before slicing.

With a sharp knife, cut the bread loaf in desired size slices. Serve fresh or you can also preserve it. For preserving place this bread in airtight container and refrigerate.

Chocolaty Banana Bread

Makes: 8-10 servings
Ingredients:
1 cup blanched almond flour
2 tablespoons cocoa powder
½ teaspoon baking soda
Pinch of salt
2 large eggs
½ cup softened almond butter
1 tablespoon melted coconut oil (at room temperature)
1 teaspoon pure vanilla extract
2 peeled and mashed medium ripe bananas
½ cup semi sweet mini dark chocolate chips
1 cup walnuts, chopped
Procedure:
Preheat the oven to 350 degrees F. Line a bread loaf pan with lightly, greased parchment paper. Keep aside. In a large mixing bowl, add almond flour, cocoa powder, baking soda and salt and mix till well combined.

In another medium mixing bowl, add eggs, almond butter, melted oil and vanilla extract and beat till well combined. Add bananas and beat till well combined. Add egg mixture into the bowl with flour mixture and mix till well combined. Gently, fold in chocolate chips and walnuts.

Now, transfer the bread mixture into prepared bread loaf pan. Place the loaf pan in heated oven. Bake for about 25 to 30 minutes or till a tooth pick inserted in the center of bread comes out clean.

Remove the loaf pan from oven and place on a wire rack. Let it cool for at least 1 to 2 hours before slicing. With a sharp knife, cut the bread loaf in desired size slices. Serve fresh or you can also preserve it. For preserving place this bread in airtight container and refrigerate.

Chocolaty Avocado Bread

Makes: 8 servings

Ingredients:
2 cups blanched almond flour
¼ cup sifted raw cacao powder
1 teaspoon baking soda
½ teaspoon salt
2 large eggs
3 tablespoons melted coconut oil (at room temperature)
3 tablespoons pure maple syrup
1 teaspoon pure vanilla extract
1½ cups peeled pitted and finely mashed avocado
2½ tablespoons coconut cream
½ cup chopped pecans
1/3 cup semi sweet mini dark chocolate chips

Procedure:
Preheat the oven to 350 degrees F. Line a bread loaf pan with lightly, greased parchment paper. Keep aside. In a large mixing bowl, add almond flour, cacao powder, baking soda and salt and mix till well combined.

In another medium mixing bowl, add eggs, oil, maple syrup and vanilla extract and beat till well combined. Add mashed avocado and coconut cream and beat till well combined. Add egg mixture into the bowl with flour mixture and mix till well combined. Gently, fold in chopped pecans and chocolate chips.

Now, transfer the bread mixture into prepared bread loaf pan. Place the loaf pan in heated oven. Bake for about 45 minutes or till a tooth pick inserted in the center of bread comes out clean.

Remove the loaf pan from oven and place on a wire rack. Let it cool for at least 1 to 2 hours before slicing. With a sharp knife, cut the bread loaf in desired size slices. Serve fresh or you can also preserve it. For preserving place this bread in airtight container and refrigerate.

Lemony Blueberry Bread

Makes: 10 servings
Ingredients:
For Bread:

2 cups blanched almond flour
1 teaspoon baking soda
Salt, to taste
½ cup melted coconut oil (at room temperature)
¼ cup full fat coconut milk
3 tablespoons agave nectar
2 eggs
2 teaspoons pure vanilla extract
¾ cup fresh blueberries
2 teaspoons freshly grated lemon zest
For Glaze:
½ tablespoon freshly squeezed lemon juice
¼ teaspoon raw honey

Procedure:
Preheat the oven to 350 degrees F. Line a bread loaf pan with lightly, greased parchment paper. Keep aside. In a large mixing bowl, add almond flour, cacao powder, baking soda and salt and mix till well combined.

In another medium mixing bowl, add oil, milk, agave nectar, eggs and vanilla extract and beat till well combined. Add egg mixture into the bowl with flour mixture and mix till well combined. Gently, fold in blueberries and lemon zest.

Now, transfer the bread mixture into prepared bread loaf pan. Place the loaf pan in heated oven. Bake for about 40 minutes or till a tooth pick inserted in the center of bread comes out clean. Remove the loaf pan from oven and place on a wire rack.

Meanwhile for glaze in a small bowl, add honey and lemon juice and beat till well combined. Pour glaze over warm bread. Let it cool for at least 1 to 2 hours before slicing. With a sharp knife, cut the bread loaf in desired size slices.

Serve fresh or you can also preserve it. For preserving place this bread in airtight container and refrigerate.

Nutty Apple Bread

Makes: 6 servings

Ingredients:

1 cup almond flour
3 tablespoons coconut flour
½ teaspoon baking soda
1 teaspoon ground cinnamon
½ teaspoon ground cardamom
¼ teaspoon salt
3 medium eggs
¼ cup melted coconut oil (at room temperature)
2 tablespoons raw honey
1 peeled, cored and finely chopped medium apple
¼ cup chopped walnuts

Procedure:

Preheat the oven to 350 degrees F. Line a bread loaf pan with lightly, greased parchment paper. Keep aside. In a large mixing bowl, add almond flour, coconut flour, baking soda, cinnamon, cardamom and salt and mix till well combined.

In another medium mixing bowl, add eggs, oil and honey and beat till well combined. Add egg mixture into the bowl with flour mixture and mix till well combined. Gently, fold in apple and walnuts.

Now, transfer the bread mixture into prepared bread loaf pan. Place the loaf pan in heated oven. Bake for about 30 to 40 minutes or till a tooth pick inserted in the center of bread comes out clean. Remove the loaf pan from oven and place on a wire rack.

Let it cool for at least 1 to 2 hours before slicing. With a sharp knife, cut the bread loaf in desired size slices. Serve fresh or you can also preserve it. For preserving place this bread in airtight container and refrigerate.

Spiced Zucchini & Banana Bread

Makes: 6-8 servings
Ingredients:
½ cup coconut flour
2 tablespoons brown sugar
1½ teaspoons baking soda
¼ teaspoons ground cinnamon
Pinch of ground cardamom
Pinch of ground ginger
Pinch of ground cloves
½ teaspoon sea salt
¼ cup melted coconut oil (at room temperature)
1½ cups peeled and mashed ripe medium bananas
2 teaspoons pure vanilla extract
1 cup grated and squeezed zucchini
1 teaspoon freshly grated orange zest

Procedure:
Preheat the oven to 350 degrees F. Line a bread loaf pan with lightly, greased parchment paper. Keep aside. In a large mixing bowl, add almond flour, brown sugar, baking soda, cinnamon, cardamom, ginger, cloves and salt and mix till well combined.

In another medium mixing bowl, add oil, bananas and vanilla extract and beat till well combined. Add egg mixture into the bowl with flour mixture and mix till well combined. Gently, fold in zucchini and orange zest.

Now, transfer the bread mixture into prepared bread loaf pan. Place the loaf pan in heated oven. Bake for about 40 to 45 minutes or till a tooth pick inserted in the center of bread comes out clean. Remove the loaf pan from oven and place on a wire rack.

Let it cool for at least 1 to 2 hours before slicing. With a sharp knife, cut the bread loaf in desired size slices. Serve fresh or you can also preserve it. For preserving place this bread in airtight container and refrigerate.

Zucchini & Carrot Bread

Makes: 6-8 servings

Ingredients:

1½ cups coconut flour

1½ teaspoons baking soda

1 teaspoon baking powder

1½ teaspoons ground cinnamon

¼ teaspoon salt

2 eggs

¾ cup raw honey

3 tablespoons melted coconut oil (at room temperature)

1 teaspoon pure vanilla extract

½ cup grated and squeezed zucchini

½ cup peeled and grated carrot

½ cup chopped walnuts

Procedure:

Preheat the oven to 375 degrees F. Line a bread loaf pan with lightly, greased parchment paper. Keep aside. In a large mixing bowl, add coconut flour, baking soda, baking powder, cinnamon and salt and mix till well combined.

In another medium mixing bowl, add eggs, honey, oil and vanilla extract and beat till well combined. Add egg mixture into the bowl with flour mixture and mix till well combined. Gently, fold in zucchini, carrot and walnut.

Now, transfer the bread mixture into prepared bread loaf pan. Place the loaf pan in heated oven. Bake for about 40 to 45 minutes or till a tooth pick inserted in the center of bread comes out clean. Remove the loaf pan from oven and place on a wire rack.

Let it cool for at least 1 to 2 hours before slicing. With a sharp knife, cut the bread loaf in desired size slices. Serve fresh or you can also preserve it. For preserving place this bread in airtight container and refrigerate.

Spiced Pumpkin Bread

Makes: 8-10 servings
Ingredients:
1½ cups almond flour
¼ cup coconut flour
¾ teaspoon baking soda
1 teaspoons ground cinnamon
¼ teaspoon ground nutmeg
¼ teaspoon ground ginger
Pinch of ground cloves
½ teaspoon sea salt
2 eggs
1/3 cup maple syrup
1 teaspoon vanilla extract
½ cup pumpkin puree

Procedure:
Preheat the oven to 350 degrees F. Line a bread loaf pan with lightly, greased parchment paper. Keep aside. In a large mixing bowl, add almond flour, coconut flour, baking soda, cinnamon, nutmeg, ginger, cloves and salt and mix till well combined.

In another medium mixing bowl, add egg, maple syrup and vanilla extract and beat well. Add pumpkin and vanilla extract and beat till well combined. Add egg mixture into bowl with flour mixture and mix till well combined.

Now, transfer the bread mixture into prepared bread loaf pan. Place the loaf pan in heated oven. Bake for about 35 minutes or till a tooth pick inserted in the center of bread comes out clean. Remove the loaf pan from oven and place on a wire rack.

Let it cool for at least 1 to 2 hours before slicing. With a sharp knife, cut the bread loaf in desired size slices. Serve fresh or you can also preserve it. For preserving place this bread in airtight container and refrigerate.

Dried Fruit& Seeds Bread

Makes: 8-10 servings

Ingredients:

¼ cup arrowroot powder

¼ teaspoon baking soda

¼ teaspoon salt

3 large eggs

¾ cup creamy almond butter (at room temperature)

2 tablespoons olive oil

1 teaspoon pure vanilla extract

1/3 cup pumpkin seeds

1/3 cup sunflower seeds

½ cup dried cranberries

¼ cup finely chopped dried apricots

1/3 cup chopped almonds, divided

Procedure:

Preheat the oven to 350 degrees F. Line a bread loaf pan with lightly, greased parchment paper. Keep aside. In a large mixing bowl, add arrowroot powder, baking soda, and salt and mix till well combined.

In another medium mixing bowl, add eggs, butter, oil and vanilla extract and beat till well combined. Add egg mixture into bowl with flour mixture and mix till well combined. Gently, fold in pumpkin seeds, sunflower seeds, cranberries, apricots and ½ cup of almonds.

Now, transfer the bread mixture into prepared bread loaf pan. Place the loaf pan in heated oven. Bake for about 40 to 50 minutes or till a tooth pick inserted in the center of bread comes out clean. Remove the loaf pan from oven and place on a wire rack.

Let it cool for at least 1 to 2 hours before slicing. With a sharp knife, cut the bread loaf in desired size slices. Serve fresh or you can also preserve it. For preserving place this bread in airtight container and refrigerate.

Nuts & Seeds Bread

Makes: 8-10 servings
Ingredients:
1½ cup blanched almond flour
¼ cup brown flax meal
¾ cup arrowroot powder
½ teaspoon baking soda
¼ teaspoon sea salt
4 large eggs
1 teaspoon apple cider vinegar
1 tablespoon agave nectar
1/3 cup pumpkin seeds
1/3 cup sunflower seeds
½ cup coarsely chopped unsalted pistachios
¼ cup coarsely chopped hazelnuts
¼ cup coarsely chopped walnuts

Procedure:

Preheat the oven to 350 degrees F. Line a bread loaf pan with lightly, greased parchment paper. Keep aside. In a large mixing bowl, add almond flour, flax meal, arrowroot powder, baking soda, and salt and mix till well combined.

In another medium mixing bowl, add eggs, vinegar and agave nectar and beat till well combined. Add egg mixture into bowl with flour mixture and mix till well combined. Gently, fold in pumpkin seeds, sunflower seeds, pistachios, hazelnuts and walnuts.

Now, transfer the bread mixture into prepared bread loaf pan. Place the loaf pan in heated oven. Bake for about 30 to 35 minutes or till a tooth pick inserted in the center of bread comes out clean. Remove the loaf pan from oven and place on a wire rack.

Let it cool for at least 1 to 2 hours before slicing. With a sharp knife, cut the bread loaf in desired size slices. Serve fresh or you can also preserve it. For preserving place this bread in airtight container and refrigerate.

Dark Caraway Seeds Bread

Makes: 8-10 servings
Ingredients:
1 cup blanched almond flour
¾ cup brown flax meal
½ teaspoon baking soda
¼ teaspoon sea salt
3 large eggs
¼ cup filtered water
2 tablespoons vegetable oil
1 teaspoon agave nectar
¾ teaspoon cream of tartar
1½ tablespoons caraway seeds

Procedure:

Preheat the oven to 350 degrees F. Line a bread loaf pan with lightly, greased parchment paper. Keep aside. In a large mixing bowl, add almond flour, flax meal, baking soda, and salt and mix till well combined.

In another medium mixing bowl, add eggs, water, oil, agave nectar and cream of tartar and beat till well combined. Add egg mixture into bowl with flour mixture and mix till well combined. Gently, fold in caraway seeds.

Now, transfer the bread mixture into prepared bread loaf pan. Place the loaf pan in heated oven. Bake for about 30 to 35 minutes or till a tooth pick inserted in the center of bread comes out clean. Remove the loaf pan from oven and place on a wire rack.

Let it cool for at least 1 to 2 hours before slicing. With a sharp knife, cut the bread loaf in desired size slices. Serve fresh or you can also preserve it. For preserving place this bread in airtight container and refrigerate.

Cheesy Pesto Bread

Makes: 10 servings
Ingredients:
2 cups blanched almond flour
7 tablespoons flax seeds meal
½ cup arrowroot powder
½ teaspoon baking soda
½ teaspoon white pepper
Salt, to taste
2 eggs
1 cup full fat coconut milk
1¾ cups shredded cheddar cheese
1/3 cup shredded parmesan cheese, divided
¼ cup prepared pesto sauce

Procedure:
Preheat the oven to 350 degrees F. Line a bread loaf pan with lightly, greased parchment paper. Keep aside. In a large mixing bowl, add almond flour, flax seeds meal, arrowroot powder, baking soda, white pepper and salt and mix till well combined.

In another medium mixing bowl, add eggs and milk and beat till well combined. Add cheddar cheese, ¼ cup of parmesan cheese and pesto and mix till well combined.

Now, transfer the bread mixture into prepared bread loaf pan. Sprinkle with remaining parmesan cheese. Place the loaf pan in heated oven. Bake for about 50 to 60 minutes or till a tooth pick inserted in the center of bread comes out clean. Remove the loaf pan from oven and place on a wire rack.

Meanwhile for glaze in a small bowl, add honey and lemon juice and beat till well combined. Pour glaze over warm bread. Let it cool for at least 1 to 2 hours before slicing. With a sharp knife, cut the bread loaf in desired size slices. Serve fresh or you can also preserve it. For preserving, wrap the loaf in paper towel and place in zip lock bag and refrigerate.

Herbed Zucchini & Carrot Bread

Makes: 14 servings
Ingredients:
¼ cup coconut flour
¼ cup ground chia seeds
¼ teaspoon baking powder
½ tablespoon crushed dried basil flakes
½ tablespoon crushed dried thyme flakes
1 tablespoon dried onion flakes
Salt and freshly ground black pepper, to taste
8 eggs
½ cup softened almond butter
½ cup grated and squeezed zucchini
½ cup peeled and grated carrot
¼ cup sunflower seeds

Procedure:

Preheat the oven to 350 degrees F. Line a bread loaf pan with lightly, greased parchment paper. Keep aside. In a large mixing bowl, add coconut flour, chia seeds, baking powder, basil, rosemary, onion flakes, salt and black pepper and mix till well combined.

In another medium mixing bowl, add eggs and butter and beat till well combined. Add egg mixture into the bowl with flour mixture and mix till well combined. Gently, fold in zucchini, carrot and sunflower seeds.

Now, transfer the bread mixture into prepared bread loaf pan. Place the loaf pan in heated oven. Bake for about 40 minutes or till a tooth pick inserted in the center of bread comes out clean. Remove the loaf pan from oven and place on a wire rack.

Let it cool for at least 1 to 2 hours before slicing. With a sharp knife, cut the bread loaf in desired size slices. Serve fresh or you can also preserve it. For preserving place this bread in airtight container and refrigerate.

Bacon & Jalapeño Pepper Bread

Makes: 6-8 servings
Ingredients:
4 (1-ounce) thick bacon slices
3 large sliced jalapeño peppers
½ cup coconut flour
¼ teaspoon baking soda
½ teaspoon sea salt
6 large eggs
½ cup melted coconut oil (at room temperature)
¼ cup filtered water

Procedure:

Preheat the oven to 400 degrees F. Lightly, grease a baking sheet. Place bacon slices and sliced jalapeño peppers into prepared baking sheet in a single layer. Roast for about 5 minutes.

Flip the sides of bacon and jalapeño peppers. Roast for about 5 minutes more. Remove from oven and cool slightly. Transfer bacon and jalapeño peppers in a food processor and pulse till chopped roughly.

In a large mixing bowl, add coconut flour, baking soda and salt and mix till well combined. In another medium mixing bowl, add eggs and oil and beat till well combined. Add egg mixture into the bowl with flour mixture and mix till well combined. Gently, fold in bacon and jalapeño peppers mixture.

Now, transfer the bread mixture into greased glass baking dish. Place the baking dish in heated oven. Bake for about 40 to 45 minutes or till a tooth pick inserted in the center of bread comes out clean. Remove the loaf pan from oven and place on a wire rack. Let it cool for at least 10 minutes. Serve warm.

Homemade Bread Recipes

Classic Sandwich Loaf

Prep time: **60 minutes**
Servings: **6**
Ingredients:
2 cups whole wheat flour
4 1/2 cups warm water
1 1/2 tablespoons salt
2/3 cup brown sugar
2/3 cup vegetable oil
10 cups bread flour
1/2 cup warm water
3 packs (25oz) active dry yeast
1/4 cup bread flour
1 tablespoon white sugar
2 cups quick cooking oats
Directions:
1. Combine 1/2 cup warm water, 1 tablespoon sugar, 1/4 cup bread flour and yeast. Let it sit for around 5 minutes.
2. Add oats, 4 1/2 water, whole wheat flour, 2/3 cup sugar, 2/3 cup of oil and salt. Mix using an electric mixer running at low speed for about 2 minutes.

3. Gradually add bread flour, half a cup at a time until dough pulls away from the bowl.
4. Grease another bowl and transfer mixture. Cover with a damp cloth and let is sit for an hour until it rises.
5. Once ready, place mixture in a greased loaf pan. Allow to rise again for another hour.
6. Place in an oven for half an hour at 350 degrees.
7. Allow to cool before serving.

Easy Banana Bread

Prep time: **70 minutes**
Servings: **6**
Ingredients:
1 1/2 cups white sugar
1/2 cup butter, softened
3 bananas, mashed
2 eggs
2 cups all-purpose flour
1/2 teaspoon baking soda
1/3 cup sour milk
1/4 teaspoon salt
1 teaspoon vanilla extract
Directions:
1. Set oven to 350 degrees.
2. Mix bananas, sugar, baking soda, eggs, salt, vanilla and milk in a bowl. Add flour and continue mixing until smooth.
3. Pour into a greased loaf pan and bake for an hour.

Homemade Whole Wheat Loaf

Prep time: 120 minutes

Servings: **6**

Ingredients:

3 cups whole wheat flour

1 packs (.25oz) fast rising yeast

1/4 cup honey

1 tablespoon butter, softened

1 teaspoon salt

1 cup warm water

1 teaspoon instant coffee granules

1 teaspoon cocoa powder

Directions:

1. Mix butter, water, instant coffee, salt, honey and cocoa powder together.
2. Slowly add 3 cups of flour, half a cup at a time. Mix using your hands.
3. Knead and add 1/2 cup of flour until dough is smooth.
4. Place dough in a bowl and cover with plastic wrap and a damp tower. Allow mixture to rise for about an hour.
5. Once ready, flatten dough and press all air out. Shape into a loaf and place on top of a baking sheet lined with parchment paper. Drape with a towel and allow to rise for another half an hour.
6. Once ready, bake for 20-30 minutes at 400 degrees.

Homemade Foccacia

Prep time: **90 minutes**
Servings: **4-6**
Ingredients:
3 1/2 cups all-purpose flour
1 teaspoon white sugar
1 teaspoon salt
1 tablespoon active dry yeast
1 cup water
2 tablespoons vegetable oil
1 egg
3 tablespoons olive oil
1 teaspoon dried rosemary, crushed
Directions:
1. Mix flour, yeast, salt and sugar.
2. Heat water and vegetable oil—add both to the mixture.
3. Crack the egg into the bowl and blend all ingredients together with an electric mixer.
4. Add 1 3/4 cup of flour.
5. Knead dough and let it sit for about 5 minutes and shape into a loaf.
6. Cover with a towel and let it sit for about half an hour.
7. Once ready, take a fork and poke through the tops.
8. Drizzle with olive oil and top with rosemary.
9. Bake for 15-25 minutes at 400 degrees.

Dinner Rolls

Prep time: 110 minutes
Servings: **12-16**
Ingredients:
3 3/4 cups bread flour, divided
1/4 cup white sugar
1/4 cup shortening
1 teaspoon salt
1 pack (.25oz) quick rising yeast
1/2 cup warm water
1/2 cup warm milk
1 egg
2 tablespoons butter, melted

Directions:
1. Combine shortening with 2 cups of flour, yeast, salt, and sugar.
2. Add milk, egg and sugar.
3. Combine all ingredients using an electric mixer.
4. Add remaining flour gradually.
5. Remove from bowl and knead on a floured surface until mixture is smooth. Form dough into a long, narrow (around 3 inch thick) loaf.
6. Cover mixture with a towel and allow to rise for about an hour.
7. Divide dough into small buns and arrange in a cake pan.
8. Brush tops with melted butter.
9. Cover again and allow to rise for another half an hour.
10. Once ready, bake for 15-20 minutes at 400 degrees.

Homemade White Bread

Prep time: 110 minutes
Servings: **8-10**
Ingredients:
2 cups warm water
2/3 cup white sugar
1 1/2 tablespoons active dry yeast
1 1/2 teaspoons salt
1/4 cup vegetable oil
6 cups bread flour
Directions:
1. Dissolve sugar in water before adding the yeast. Keep whisking until mixture achieves a creamy foam consistency.
2. Add salt and oil into the mixture and gradually add flour, half a cup at a time.
3. Knead on a floured surface. Transfer mixture to a greased bowl and cover with damp cloth.
4. Allow to rise for about an hour.
5. Press dough to remove air from the dough and knead.
6. Divide dough in half and shape into loaves. Cover both and allow to rise for another half an hour.
7. Bake for half an hour at 350 degrees.

Zucchini And Walnut Loaf

Prep time: **70 minutes**
Servings: **8-10**
Ingredients:
3 cups all-purpose flour
1 teaspoon salt
1 teaspoon baking soda
1 teaspoon baking powder
3 teaspoons ground cinnamon
3 eggs
1 cup vegetable oil
2 1/4 cups white sugar
3 teaspoons vanilla extract
2 cups grated zucchini
1 cup chopped walnuts

Directions:
1. Set oven to 325 degrees.
2. Combine salt, baking powder, flour, baking soda and cinnamon together in a bowl.
3. In another bowl, mix eggs, oil, sugar and vanilla.
4. Combine both together and mix until smooth.
5. Add zucchini and nuts and mix thoroughly.
6. Pour into a bread tin and bake for 40-60 minutes.

Homemade French Baguette

Prep time: 160 minutes
Servings: **6-10**
Ingredients:
6 cups all-purpose flour
 2 1/2 packs (.25oz) active dry yeast
 1 1/2 teaspoons salt
 2 cups warm water
 1 tablespoon cornmeal
 1 egg white
 1 tablespoon water
Directions:
1. Mix 2 cups of flour, salt and yeast.
2. Add water and beat until well blended.
3. Add remaining flour until you achieve an elastic dough consistency.
4. On a floured surface, knead dough and let it sit for about an hour to rise, while covered with a cloth.
5. Once ready, punch the dough down and divide in two. Shape into narrow loaves.
6. Place on a greased baking sheet and sprinkle with cornmeal.
7. Beat egg whites with water and brush mixture onto the loaves.
8. Allow loaves to rise for another 40 minutes. Brush with egg white mixture again.
9. Bake for 20 minutes at 375 degrees.

Apple Walnut Loaf

Prep time: 120 minutes
Servings: **4-6**
Ingredients:
3 cups all-purpose flour
1 teaspoon baking soda
1 teaspoon salt
1 cup chopped walnuts
3 cups apples - peeled, cored, and chopped
1 cup vegetable oil
2 cups white sugar
3 eggs, beaten
2 teaspoons ground cinnamon
Directions:
1. Set oven to 300 degrees.
2. Combine baking soda with flour, salt, walnuts and apples.
3. In another bowl, combine sugar, oil, cinnamon and eggs.
4. Combine both and mix together.
5. Divide batter into two, greased loaf pans and place in the oven.
6. Bake for 90 minutes.

Homemade Ciabatta

Prep time: 120 minutes
Servings: **4-6**
Ingredients:
1 1/2 cups water
1 1/2 teaspoons salt
1 teaspoon white sugar
1 tablespoon olive oil
3 1/4 cups bread flour
1 1/2 teaspoons bread machine yeast
Directions:
1. Using a bread machine, combine all ingredients into the pan and select dough cycle.
2. Take the dough and cover with a towel. Allow to rest for 15 minutes.
3. Divide dough in two and form into loaves.
4. Cover and allow to rise for around 45 minutes.
5. Set oven to 425 degrees and bake for 25-30 minutes.

Western Fried Bread

Prep time: **90 minutes**
Servings: **8**
Ingredients:
1/2 cup boiling water
3/4 cup cold milk
1 teaspoon white sugar
1 1/2 teaspoons active dry yeast
1 egg, beaten
2 tablespoons butter, melted and cooled
1/4 teaspoon salt
1/4 teaspoon ground nutmeg
4 cups all-purpose flour
Directions:
1. Combine milk, sugar and water.
2. Add yeast and allow to stand for 5 minutes.
3. Combine butter and egg into the mixture.
4. Add nutmeg, salt and 2 cups of flour.
5. Mix until well blended.
6. Knead dough on a floured surface for 10 minutes and cover with a towel. Allow to rise for about an hour.
7. Once ready, divide dough into 8 equal portions. Cover and let it rest for another 20 minutes.
8. Once ready, fry each piece for about a minute on each side.
9. Serve immediately.

Warm Dill Loaf

Prep time: **3 hours**
Servings: **6-8**
Ingredients:
1 pack (.25) active dry yeast
1/4 cup warm water
1 pinch white sugar
1 cup cottage cheese
1 tablespoon margarine
2 tablespoons white sugar
2 teaspoons dried dill
1 teaspoon dried minced onion
1 teaspoon salt
1/4 teaspoon baking soda
1 egg
2 1/4 cups all-purpose flour
1 tablespoon margarine, melted
1 teaspoon kosher salt

Directions:
1. Combine water, yeast and a pinch of sugar. Set aside.
2. In a sauce pan, mix cottage cheese and margarine until melted.
3. Remove from heat and add remaining sugar, dill seed and herbs, onion flakes, baking soda and salt.
4. Add egg and yeast mixture.
5. Add flour and mix well.
6. Place dough on a greased bowl and cover. Allow to rise for about an hour.
7. Punch dough to remove air and place into a bread tin.
8. Cover and allow to rise again for about 40 minutes.
9. Bake for 50 minutes in an oven set at 350 degrees.

Homemade Olive Bread Bites

Prep time: 120 minutes
Servings: **6-8**
Ingredients:
2 1/2 cups warm water
2 tablespoons active dry yeast
1 teaspoon molasses
2 tablespoons olive oil
1 tablespoon salt
7 1/2 cups bread flour
1 cup kalamata olives, pitted and chopped
2 tablespoons chopped fresh rosemary
1 tablespoon sesame seeds

Directions:
1. Combine water and molasses and set aside until mixture becomes foamy and creamy.
2. Add salt and olive oil; gradually add flour, one cup at a time.
3. Add herbs and olives.
4. Place dough on a floured surface and knead until it becomes elastic.
5. Transfer to a greased bowl and cover with a towel. Allow to rise for about an hour.
6. Once ready, press down to remove air and divide into two. Form into loaves and place on a baking sheet.
7. Spray cold water on the loaves and sprinkle with sesame seeds. Cover and allow to rise for half an hour.
8. Bake for half an hour at 400 degrees.

Melted Muenster Bun

Prep time: **80 minutes**
Servings: **6**
Ingredients:
3 1/2 teaspoons white sugar
2 teaspoons salt
1 tablespoon active dry yeast
4 cups all-purpose flour
1/2 cup margarine
1 cup milk
1 egg
1 egg yolk
2 pounds Muenster cheese, shredded
1 egg white, beaten
2 tablespoons whole blanched almonds
Directions:
1. Combine butter and milk in a skillet over low heat.
2. IN a bowl, combine yeast, sugar and salt. Add milk mixture. Beat mixture for about 2 minutes.
3. Gradually add 1 cup of flour while beating until you achieve a soft dough.
4. Place dough on a floured surface and knead until smooth. Cover and allow to rest for 15 minutes.
5. Combine egg and egg yolk with shredded cheese.
6. Once dough is ready, take a rolling pin and roll dough flat.
7. Place cheese mixture in the middle and fold dough around it. Pinch seams to seal and cover with towel while you let it rest for about 10 minutes.
8. Once ready, brush with egg white and sprinkle with blanched almonds.
9. Bake for an hour at 350 degrees.

Mango Walnut Loaf

Prep time: **70 minutes**
Servings: **6**
Ingredients:
2 cups all-purpose flour
2 teaspoons baking soda
2 teaspoons ground cinnamon
1/2 teaspoon salt
3 eggs
3/4 cup softened butter
1 1/4 cups white sugar
1 teaspoon vanilla extract
2 cups chopped mango
1/2 cup shredded coconut
1/4 cup chopped walnuts
Directions:
1. Set oven to 350 degrees.
2. Combine cinnamon with flour, salt and baking soda. Create a well in the middle of the dry ingredients.
3. Combine butter, vanilla extract, butter, sugar and eggs in another bowl. Once smooth, add coconut, mango and walnuts. Pour mixture into the well.
4. Combine all ingredients together and let it rest for 20 minutes.
5. Transfer dough into a loaf tin and bake for an hour in the oven.

Homemade Herbed Loaf

Prep time: **60 minutes**
Servings: **8**
Ingredients:
- 1/4 cup warm water
- 2 tablespoons margarine
- 3/4 cup milk
- 1 egg
- 1 teaspoon dried parsley
- 1 1/2 teaspoons salt
- 1/2 teaspoon ground nutmeg
- 1 teaspoon rubbed sage
- 2 teaspoons celery seed
- 3 cups bread flour
- 2 tablespoons white sugar
- 1 teaspoon active dry yeast

Directions:
1. Combine all ingredients in a bread machine and follow instructions.
2. Once ready, knead dough and cover with a damp towel. Allow to rise about an hour.
3. Once ready, place dough in a bread tin and bake at 400 degrees for 40 minutes.

Homemade Buttermilk Cornbread

Prep time: **60 minutes**
Servings: **8**
Ingredients:
1/2 cup butter
2/3 cup white sugar
2 eggs
1 cup buttermilk
1/2 teaspoon baking soda
1 cup cornmeal
1 cup all-purpose flour
1/2 teaspoon salt
Directions:
1. Set oven to 375 degrees.
2. Melt sugar over low heat and add sugar.
3. Add eggs and beat into the mixture until well blended.
4. Add baking soda and buttermilk; mix in cornmeal, flour and salt. Once smooth, pour into a square baking pan.
5. Bake for 30-40 minutes.

Honey Bun

Prep time: 120 minutes

Servings: **6-8**

Ingredients:

1 1/4 cups warm water
2 tablespoons molasses
2 tablespoons honey
1 envelope active dry yeast
2 tablespoons canola oil
2 cups unbleached all-purpose flour
1 cup whole wheat flour
1 1/2 teaspoons sea salt
3 tablespoons raw pumpkin seeds
2 tablespoons raw sunflower seeds
1 tablespoon poppy seeds
2 tablespoons millet seed
3 tablespoons malted barley flour
1 tablespoon wheat gluten
1 egg white, beaten
1 teaspoon millet seed

Directions:

1. Combine molasses, water, yeast and honey. Let it rest and add oil.
2. Combine all dry ingredients together.
3. Gradually stir together dry ingredients with the yeast mixture and mix well.
4. Take dough and knead for 10 minutes on a floured surface. Cover with a towel and let it rise for an hour.
5. Shape into a loaf and place on a baking sheet. Cover and allow to rise for another 40 minutes.
6. Set oven to 375 degrees.
7. Brush dough with egg white and place in the oven. Bake for 45 minutes.

Cereal Wheat Breakfast Loaf

Prep time: 120 minutes
Servings: **5-10**
Ingredients:
1 cup bite size frosted wheat cereal
1 cup brown sugar
1/2 cup shortening
1 teaspoon salt
1 cup boiling water
2 packs (.25oz) active dry yeast
1 cup warm water
2 eggs
6 cups bread flour

Directions:
1. Combine brown sugar, shortening and salt and boiling water.
2. Dissolve yeast in water and allow to stand until creamy. Combine with the yeast mixture.
3. Add eggs and 2 cups of flour and mix until smooth. Gradually add remaining flour, half a cup at a time.
4. Transfer mixture to a floured surface and knead until elastic.
5. Place in a greased bowl and cover until dough rises—about an hour.
6. Punch dough to remove air and shape into two loaves. Cover and allow to rise for another 40 minutes.
7. Bake for half an hour at 350 degrees.

Homemade Brown Bread

Prep time: 120 minutes
Servings: **4-6**
Ingredients:
1 cup bread flour
1 cup whole wheat flour
1 cup cornmeal
1 cup molasses
2 cups water
1 teaspoon baking soda
1 teaspoon salt
Directions:
1. Combine wheat flour, bread flour, cornmeal and baking soda.
2. Add molasses and water. Mix thoroughly.
3. Pour into a loaf pan and place in a steamer. Cover and steam over low heat for 1 hour and 45 minutes.

CPSIA information can be obtained
at www.ICGtesting.com
Printed in the USA
BVHW022341011222
653288BV00009B/162